I0824221

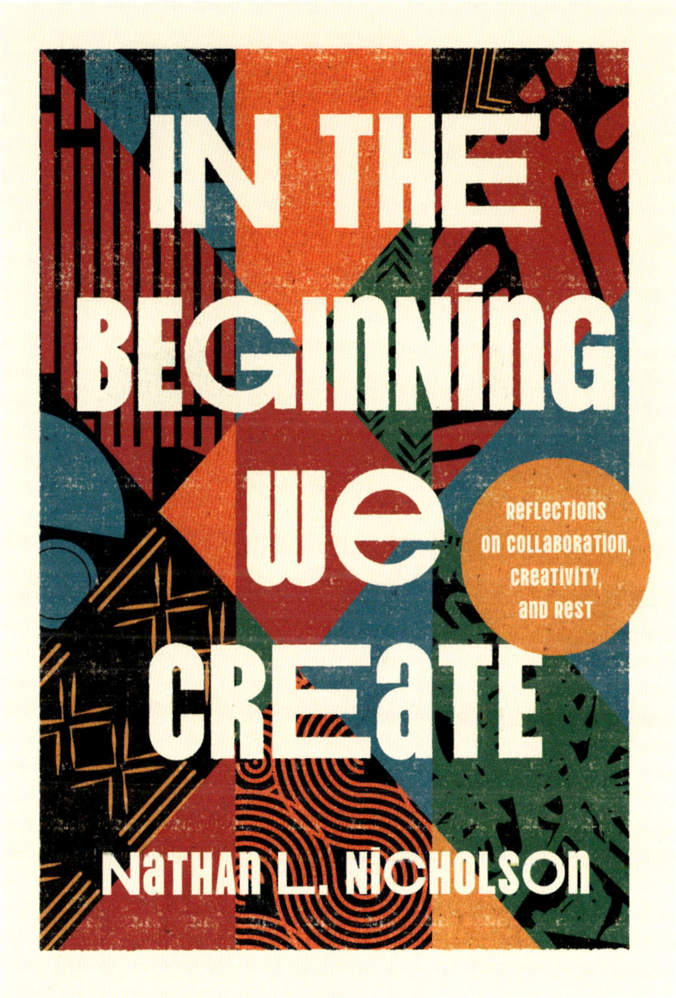

IN THE BEGINNING WE CREATE

REFLECTIONS ON COLLABORATION, CREATIVITY, AND REST

NATHAN L. NICHOLSON

An imprint of InterVarsity Press
Downers Grove, Illinois

For Atlas

InterVarsity Press
P.O. Box 1400 | Downers Grove, IL 60515-1426
ivpress.com | email@ivpress.com

InterVarsity Press® is the publishing division of InterVarsity Christian Fellowship/USA®. For more information, visit intervarsity.org.

Cover design: Faceout Studio, Molly von Borstel
Interior design: Jeanna Wiggins
Images: © Tama2u and © craftlove via Shutterstock

ISBN 978-1-5140-1266-6 (print) | ISBN 978-1-5140-1267-3 (digital)
Printed in Colombia ♾

Library of Congress Cataloging-in-Publication Data
A catalog record for this book is available from the Library of Congress.

8 7 6 5 4 3 2 1 | 31 30 29 28 27 26

CONTENTS

INTRODUCTION

I know I have an artistic passion, but what do I do with it?

I know I have creative ability, but how do I harness it?

How do I make my God-given creative gifts effective?

If you're asking yourself these questions, this book is for you. Perhaps you're a painter, photographer, graphic designer, sculptor, or other kind of visual artist. Maybe you're a musician, producer, or music director. You might be a writer, speaker, clothing designer, florist, or actor. Maybe you get paid for your creations, or maybe art is something you do for fun or a sense of fulfillment. Whatever you do, creativity is part of who you are.

This book is for:

- Creative people who don't think that they are "creators."
- People who are just starting in their creative journey and need some guidance.
- People who have been on this journey of creative discovery for a while and need some refreshment.

Whoever you are, if you have the creative light burning within you, I'd like to fan your flame and keep it healthy. We could all learn from the steps God used to create us.

God is the ultimate Creator, and his creative abilities are unmatched. This book explores God's creative process and how we can emulate it in what he has gifted us to do. The book of Genesis will form the biblical foundation of our exploration. We'll take brief excursions into other books of the Bible, but most chapters will return to Genesis. I've found a lot of direction and inspiration for my artistic journey in this book of the Bible, especially the story of God creating the universe, and I want to share what I've learned with you.

In addition to the book of Genesis, three big themes have helped me grow into the artist I am today: collaboration with God and with other creative people, the idea that human creativity is a reflection of God's work in creation, and the importance of rest in the life of a creative person. Each of these themes has its own chapter, but all three are so central to the way I think about art that they feature in other chapters as well.

You may be wondering who I am and what led me to write this book. I'm an artist, filmmaker, photographer, designer, and Christian minister. I'm a creator. I create to glorify God. I love creating because it's fun and brings me a great sense of joy and fulfillment. It's a huge part of my purpose. Through my creations, I aim to bring people together and inspire them to live. In many of my works, I make the skin tones a deep, sublime black to represent a sense of reverence. In other pieces, I make the skin a uniform grayscale—a nod to the uniqueness of Black people, which is sometimes lost in assumed stereotypes. Despite these less-than-vibrant skin tones, the beauty of the composition and individuality of their skin shines through.

This book features original pieces I have created. You can think of them as checkpoints on your creative journey through this text. I'd like to collaborate with you within these pages. Allow this book to be a spark for your creativity. Some artworks in this book are composite pieces in which I bring elements together to make something beautiful. Others are Paper Portraits, inspired by photos I took during a photo shoot or other event. While not every chapter has a corresponding piece of art, there are series of artworks placed throughout the chapters.

There are twenty-one chapters in this book. I invite you to take it all in on a consistent schedule. That may mean reading one chapter a day over twenty-one days, or one chapter every other day, or one per week—whatever is comfortable for you. You may also want to read it with a partner or a group and be inspired in collaboration. Each chapter contains a prompt to spur you to creative action. If you act on the prompt, reflect on the artwork interspersed among the chapters, and keep an open mind and heart, you will be on your way to a transformative experience of creativity.

Are you ready to create? Let's begin!

start from nothing

DIGITAL ABSTRACTS

This work is a combination of digital paint and ink strokes, along with preexisting shapes, primarily made on my iPad in Procreate. These pieces are an interpretation of what I felt in the moment. Some are inspired by places I traveled to between 2021 and 2023, and others are inspired by songs and sermons I have listened to.

1

CREATED FOR CREATIVITY

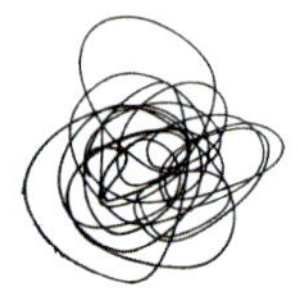

BEFORE THE REIGN of *The Oprah Winfrey Show*, Phil Donahue was king of daytime TV ratings. I saw a clip of Bob Ross on *The Phil Donahue Show* from 1994. Donahue yelled in his own annoying and provocative way to Ross, "Say out loud your work will never hang in a museum, Bob!" Ross's response was, "I'm trying to teach people a form of art that anybody can do. This art is for anyone who's ever wanted to put a dream on canvas. It's not traditional art, it's not fine art, and I don't try to tell anybody it is." Ross wanted to open up the realm of creativity in a way that was accessible to millions. For eleven years, his program *The Joy of Painting* did just that. He provided people with the opportunity to complete a painting by the end of the show. He creatively found a way to bring a one-on-one teaching session to millions of students at home.[1]

Why was Ross's method so appealing to so many people? Why were millions of people—career artists and hobbyists alike—so enamored with the idea of creating art?

It's tough to make definitive statements about all of humanity, but we can find clues about our creative impulse in the Bible's account of creation. We are creative because we were made in the image of our Creator.

GOD IS CREATIVE

"In the beginning God created" (Genesis 1:1). The Hebrew word translated as *created* is a verb that refers to creating something out of nothing. It is only used to describe God's kind of creation, which brings something out of nothing, or *ex nihilo*. This is an exclusive function of God's omnipotence. God stepped out on nothing, spoke to nothing, and consulted with no one but himself—and from that nothing he created everything. He spoke from eternity, and time began. In the Bible God is referenced as the ultimate Creator (Genesis 1:1; Isaiah 40:28). The first thing we learn about God is that he is and was in the beginning, and the second thing we learn about God is that he creates. I find it fascinating that one of the very first attributes of God we encounter is his creativity. Our God creates. And as his intelligent design, made in his image, we also create. Creativity is godly. Just as we inherit certain traits from our natural parents, we inherit our creative impulse from God.

God's creative process provides a template for everything that we create. He determined the starting point. He set aside time. We do not need to look too far into Genesis before we find God's template for creating effectively.

> In the beginning God created the heavens and the earth. Now the earth was formless and empty, darkness was over the surface of the deep, and the Spirit of God was hovering over the waters. And God said, "Let there be light," and there was light. God saw that the light was good, and he separated the light from the darkness. God called the light "day," and the darkness he called "night." And there was evening, and there was morning—the first day. (Genesis 1:1-5)

The earth needed order, so God established seasons, created a hierarchy, and implemented systems. The universe wasn't a blank canvas; rather, it was something raw that God placed into perfect order. This scriptural template shows how God focused on the big details first and then on the more intricate details throughout the process. He made the heavens and the earth first. We can think of these as the frames of his artistic masterpiece. If we continue reading, we see that he then filled the frames with masterful creativity and detail, color, and texture. Light. Plants. Sun. Moon. Stars. Birds. Land animals. And God's most creative and detailed work—humanity.

Consider the creation of humankind for a moment. God drew up the plans for his creation of Adam when he said, "Let us make mankind in our image, in our likeness" (Genesis 1:26). Being made in God's image entails so much more than just the physical aspect. We are made in his image and likeness as spiritual and moral beings. Thinking and feeling beings. Creative beings. We as humans are an original

design by God, but in our originality, we also see that God used himself as the template in our creation.

WE GET OUR CREATIVITY FROM GOD

Creativity is an expression of intimate thought, marrying our gifts and passions with our past experiences and current ideas. Creativity helps to carry thoughts from ideas to reality and dreams to fruition. It is an artistic expression that originates with a simple concept and ends with a beautiful creation. It is the manifestation of God's gift of inspiration, freedom of thought, and the courage to try new things. Creativity also adds flavor to life; it expresses originality, challenging the conventional and unleashing our imagination. It is the splash of color on a blank canvas, the spark that breathes new life into the plain and uninspiring. It is not simply artistry, but it also provides solutions to problems with flair and poised balance. Creativity is where innovation and imagination meet to give birth to something new. Our creativity allows us to transform ideas into real works of art. Innovation is a freeing act of courage that enables you to set trends. You are not simply a thermometer. You are a thermostat, setting trends and seeking to gain new ground in what has never been done or even known before. People may not understand at first, but don't let that distract you. Though it's a new idea, somehow it makes perfect sense, leaving other people to wonder, *Why didn't I think of that?*

We inherited this trait from our heavenly Father. When we express our creativity, we are, in effect, collaborating with God to bring more beauty into the world. What would life be without creativity?

No matter the creative discipline we use, we can offer our creativity back to God. We can become a worship leader without a mic or a worshiper equipped with creative acumen whose instrument is a laptop, paintbrush, camera, clay, pen, pencil, or Conté crayon. No matter the avenue, we can render our services to the glory of God, making our mark one project at a time.

God is perfect, and he created everything with perfection. Although we were also created to create, we are imperfect, and our creations will not always turn out perfectly. That's okay. There's peace in knowing that when we create, we can imitate God. We simply have to start with the framework and home in on the details later.

By offering our creativity to God, we give back to him what he has given us in a spirit of worship. What do you create? How do you give it back to him?

RESPONSE

This is your opportunity and excuse to create something new. Do you have an idea for a creative project? Before the day is done, take one practical step toward turning that idea into a reality.

TIME IS WAITING ON YOU TO START

2 COLLABORATION

When I think of creative collaboration, the first thing I think about is Bauhaus. Not only is it the name of one of my favorite fonts, it was also a German art movement from 1919 to 1933 as well as an art school that taught a holistic way of creating. The methodology behind Bauhaus was to blend multiple artistic practices into one approach. The students who attended this school were encouraged to be creative in every aspect of life. It was a new way of learning that did away with traditional academic norms. The architect Walter Gropius headed up the school, and his philosophy was based on American architect Louis Sullivan's guiding principle: "Form follows function."[2]

At Bauhaus, they collaborated and prioritized intention and purpose. The goal of collaboration is to meld different methods together for an intentional outcome. Collaboration allows diverse personalities to sit at the creative table together. Take a project with two artists who have varying experience and skill levels. The less experienced person can glean wisdom from the veteran, and the established creative can lend their expertise and reputation to validate the other person's work. The most effective collaboration happens among those with different skill sets. When was the last time you saw a team solely made up of directors release a movie together? If there's going to be a smooth production from start to finish, there needs to be diversity of thought, skill, and perspective. A team of individuals needs to operate in different functions while still working together as one to accomplish the task.

ELEVATE BLACK VOICES

In 2024 I started an ongoing short-form interview documentary series titled *Elevate Black Voices*. The series encourages Black people to use and value their voice as a necessity. The interviews are from the perspective of only those who are interviewed, allowing their voices to emerge in a way that is undeniable. This series not only uplifts their physical voices but also empowers them to tell their stories and use their expertise to inform others. It highlights the uniqueness of Black people and the need for our contributions in every arena that we occupy.

The idea for this collaborative series started on a Sunday afternoon after church when I took out my camera and asked my wife, "What does being Black mean to you?" I also interviewed some great people who are part of my community. I figured I could collaborate with these talented people to make something great and tell their story.

TRINITARIAN COLLABORATION

We can learn about the beauty and importance of collaboration when we look at Scripture. God is one God in three persons. He is Elohim, the all-powerful One, the Creator of the universe. God consulted, communicated, and collaborated among himself to create. So God the Father, God the Son—Jesus, the Word made flesh who dwelt among us

(John 1:1-3, 14)—and God the Holy Ghost, who is our helper and the manifestation of God's will and power on earth, brought forth creation as three persons in one.

Don't think of the concept as 1 + 1 + 1 = 3, but rather 1 x 1 x 1 = 1.[3] While the term *Trinity* is not found in Scripture, the theme and precept of the triune God is all throughout Scripture. There are over sixty Scriptures that support this concept of the triune Godhead. He *is* Father, he *is* Son, he *is* Holy Ghost. So God collaborates. God fellowships with himself and has enjoyed this fellowship for all of eternity.

Humanity's creation also highlights how positively God sees and uses creative collaboration. The first mention of the creation of a human in Scripture points to a collaborative effort: "Let *us* make man."

In trinitarian collaboration, God created heaven and said it was good. He created the earth and everything in it and said it was good. He took pleasure in affirming the value of what he had made. But there was one thing that God said was not good—for man to be alone. Though the woman came from a man in a literal sense—his rib—on his own he had no companionship, no partnership, no collaboration, and he could not reproduce by himself. Though he had an audience with God, something was missing. As much as we should cherish God's company, there is also value in human connection. God's solution was to make a helper for Adam. Not only would she be his helpmate and wife, but she would also be a collaborator, a teammate, and a partner. Collaboration goes beyond God's plan for marriage or family life; it is an important element in accomplishing creative goals.

WE ALL NEED HELP

Collaboration is so important. In many cases, with big projects, it is difficult to do everything alone. It takes partnership. Flying solo often works, but having partnership unlocks bigger possibilities for expansion.

When collaborating, it is important for every party to actively participate to bring ideas to life. We can depend on one another to create a finished product. The process itself makes partnership the focus of the operation. We make ourselves vulnerable. We collaborate with one another to make great things, and what we create is ultimately a collaboration with God. As the Holy Spirit inspires us to create, we put our creation out into the world.

Collaborating with individuals of different skill sets differs from collaborating with those who have similar skill sets. The latter is what I like to call "communal collaboration," which is about working with people with similar skills to solve the puzzle together and draw inspiration from one another.

Those in the same discipline need community to maintain morale, stay motivated, remain fully engaged, and stay accountable to the creative process. While we don't have to be friends to share in communal collaboration, we develop a sense of camaraderie when we look into the eyes of someone who has gone where we've gone. The intimacy of shared workmanship fosters openness and honesty with one another, and spending time in the same space and in proximity forges a bond. Our shared history alone creates a lasting connection.

If you make the decision to be in community, you have to be intentional about building one. Just know that you are inviting people to the table and into your business. In this age of virtual connection that we live in, community has become less about proximity and more about shared values. But I see the value of both models. Find your circle, whether online or among places and institutions where creative people gather. At the same time, it's important to find those people in proximity as well. Ultimately, one doesn't have to live in close quarters to display community values. To operate in community means that you act in the interest of the whole community.

RESPONSE

Find collaborators! First, plan to participate in a project with at least one other person. Collaborate with someone who does something different from you. Figure out a way you can work together for a short-term common goal.

Second, take part in some communal collaboration. Reach out to someone of the same discipline and skill set on social media or locally. You have the freedom to work on a project together, but it's more important that you walk alongside one another. Meet up quarterly if you can.

3

WORKMANSHIP

Design is all around us and encompasses a great many things. Everything has been intentionally created by a designer who took time to craft it. Whatever we use, see, and read was designed. Nothing has come to exist by accident or happenstance. Someone either saw a need and created something to meet it or encountered a problem and created something to solve it.

Scripture says God created every creeping thing. Let that sink in for a second. There are between two and thirty million known insect species in the world.[4] Out of those, 40 percent are beetle species. According to Britannica, there are over three hundred thousand known beetle species. Out of those, the firefly is one known soft-bodied beetle species. There are over twenty thousand known firefly species in existence.[5] God handcrafted every one of those species down to the most minute detail. He is truly a master craftsman, and every living thing on earth testifies to his craftsmanship.

As part of creation, we humans are his workmanship. Created by his skilled and ancient hands. Crafted by eternal wisdom. Founded upon the word of his power. When we look at the process of creation, we see that everything else was spoken into existence: "And God said,

'Let there be light'" (Genesis 1:3). The phrase "God said" is used ten times in the account of creation. But when it came to Adam, God decided to get his hands dirty: "And the Lord God formed man of the dust of the ground, and breathed into his nostrils the breath of life; and man became a living soul" (Genesis 2:7 KJV).

Adam was shaped as a masterpiece from the dust of the ground—dust that bears God's mark. This dust was held together because of the breath of life breathed into Adam's nostrils. We were designed with incredible detail, down to the numbering of our hairs. Our God is so concerned with detail that he orchestrates the bottling of our tears. David used this imagery when illustrating God's care for us in Psalm 56:8. The love and care God shows us lets us know his level of attentiveness.

GET YOUR HANDS DIRTY

There is no greater feeling than using raw materials to make something with the work of your hands. The sweat equity alone makes it special. Toiling with ingenuity and uncertainty, putting forth effort to problem solve and shape a creation from abstraction to completion, makes the result that much more satisfying.

Passionate, skilled workmanship requires getting your hands dirty. I say this figuratively when it comes to God's creative process, but I also mean it quite literally. There is something about seeing raw materials transform before your very eyes. The active nature of it all is therapeutic. Having to wash your hands and pick grime out of your fingernails makes you invested in the process. That is just what God did. In his creative process, he got his hands dirty. He formed man from the dust of the ground. Think of the masterpiece that humankind is in all of our functions, potentials, and capabilities. We were not made as a standalone work of art but rather as a piece that would reproduce of its own kind from the beginning of our time until now.

We are not only one of God's prized creations, but we are also a creation with the power to create ourselves. We create in our own realm and within the parameters that God has put in place, possessing the power and ingenuity to cultivate all else that he has created. With varying personalities, passions, and arrays of color, we are of different cultures and tongues and inhabit every corner of the earth. What a mighty, thoughtful, and creative God.

God's proficiency should encourage us to master our creative technique so that we know it like the back of our hand. Let the skillful works flow through your hands.

Ephesians 2:10 says that we are Christ's workmanship, meaning we ourselves are a work of art, a skillful masterpiece crafted by the hand of God. The sheer fact that God the all-supreme, omnipotent, and ageless Spirit crafted our carefully formulated existence is mind-blowing. Not only that, he breathed the breath of life into us. He didn't choose gears or some kind of inanimate mechanism to give us life. Rather, the same breath that he breathed into Adam's nostrils flows through our lungs. That life has been passed down from generation to generation as a heritage of divine workmanship.

TECHNIQUE

Processes are important to creative workmanship and serve as a recipe for success. Some processes are like a template. Others, like scripted instructions with a checklist, are less fluid. God's whole process was schematic. To know systems is to recognize patterns. There is a reason the chocolate, caramel, and strawberry syrup that you put on your ice cream looks almost identical with varying colors.

It is a system, a pattern that works well within a framework. It becomes an easily identifiable language pointing back to the efficiency of your workmanship. Every such pattern tells a story.

Technique is necessary if you wish to produce similar results. Those who value the technical side will appreciate knowing your process, but what matters most are the results because everyone will see the final product of your workmanship.

RESPONSE

Investigate alternative methods, software, and tools to do what you already do well. Get your hands dirty. Doing so will enhance your workmanship.

DEFINE

CUSTOM-MADE

GROWING UP, WHAT I CHERISHED most about WWE video games was the ability to create a character. My brothers and their best friend knew that if I wanted to create a character, it was going to take a while. I took my time to craft every detail to perfection, mixing entrance music with character motion and outfits. Little did I know that the pleasure I took in creating characters would serve as a precursor to my love for graphic design and digital media. Much of the software I use today was introduced to me at an early age. When it came time to learn the industry standard software and edit video and audio, I was not frazzled because it looked familiar.

Much like the way I crafted characters in my childhood video game, I have, in a way, "created" myself as an artist. Of course, I don't mean this in any literal sense—God is my only true Creator. But just as I would add features to my WWE characters, I have spent years outfitting myself with new artistic skills and proficiencies. This process of "self-creation" is important for every artist, and it's another way for us to emulate God's creative power.

When God formed Adam from the dust, I imagine him obsessing over every detail—the intricate facial features, the complexities of the internal organs, the musculature and mobility, the miraculous way Adam's genetic material would give rise to billions upon billions of unique humans. As creative people, we can imagine ourselves carefully crafting our artistic identity.

TRY NEW THINGS

When I started my brick-and-mortar creative journey, I had to do things that didn't necessarily fit my skill set but that contributed to the expansion of my skill set. What I acquired along the way enhanced me and made me a well-rounded creative professional.

Being a production artist enabled me to be fast on my feet. As a digital media specialist, I had to bounce around and do a little bit of everything. I needed to make quick ad hoc marketing pieces for differently branded car dealerships. I also assumed the role of a graphic artist because of my graphic design work. Things like clipping images out of backgrounds prepared me to place elements together. Extracting elements from images serve as a fundamental part of design and graphic art. This and other repetitious tasks that seemed mundane at the time paid off in the long run. They served as conditioning for what I would go on to do on my own terms. It all shaped me into a better artist.

The journey is often frustrating because you'll find yourself learning new skills before it seems like you've mastered your current ones. In that case, it's not so much about attaining mastery as it is about being versatile and useful. What good is it to master one skill if you lack the willingness to cross over into other disciplines to get the job done? What good does it serve a graphic designer to know only one program? I started my design journey by learning Adobe Photoshop, which developed into a frustrating introduction to Illustrator. That then led me to dive into InDesign, which I literally had to learn on the job. Like most designers I know who have jumped ship, I only started doing photography because I was dissatisfied with the photos people provided me to create designs with. And I only started doing video because while shooting an event, the videographer couldn't make it.

I often find myself in disbelief when I consider how some of my creative skills have developed over the years. Things I found challenging have become second nature. Your creative utility belt should be as endless and resourceful as Robin's in the 1960s version of the *Batman* TV series. Like when Batman encounters a shark and Robin just happens to have a spray can of shark repellent handy, you need to be ready for anything. I welcome opportunities to try new things and new avenues in which to create because it's all part of the process of creating myself.

When learning new things, tutorials should be your best friend. YouTube was launched when I was a freshman in high school. Want to know a three-ingredient cookie recipe? Go to YouTube. Want to fix an air leak in your tire? Go to YouTube. People visit YouTube to be educated and informed. If you have a question, trust that someone else has asked it before you. Both extensive and bite-sized tutorials are a mainstay of the platform. Half of what I've learned creatively has come from a tutorial.

Part of creating yourself is taking advantage of teaching moments. They are not always labeled or accompanied by a syllabus, but sense when something you witness can increase your capacity to create. Take those moments as they come. What associations are you a part of? How many conferences have you attended that fostered growth? You can't afford to be passive when it comes to developing new skills that will enrich you. It is in those places that small conversations and icebreakers turn into meaningful relationships. Put yourself out there and position yourself for growth. Leverage the opportunities around you. If you don't live in a location where events, conferences, and clubs exist, maybe you need to build something that solves the growth problem for others. And don't underestimate the effectiveness of virtual events and seminars. When you connect with others—whether they are like-minded people or those who challenge you to think differently—they can help you develop your artistic identity. The age of the internet makes this even easier. Some of the most collaborative and encouraging people in my life who support my art are social media friends I've never met in person. Don't get me wrong, I have a core group of people who support me locally, but I expand community online at a much faster rate.

When it comes to creating yourself, versatility is key. It behooves you to try, even when uncertainty and inexperience try to hold you captive as a prisoner in a creative mold. Creativity can send you on a journey of discovery. Rather than having it all planned out in your head, step out of the boat into endless possibilities.

RESPONSE

Try something new today, maybe a new artform or a new skill within an artform you're already familiar with. That new thing just might become part of your artistic identity.

FIND *IT*

5

ORIGINALITY

Keenen Ivory Wayans said that when he and Robert Townsend made the movie *Hollywood Shuffle*,[6] ignorance was their greatest asset.[7] They were able to do their thing on their own terms. The film was a foundation for a certain style of comedy that would influence the next forty years of filmmaking and countless other films and comedians. If these two legends had not stepped forward at the time they did, the world would be devoid of the many actors and comedians they were able to discover. So many legends and works of art would not exist without these two letting their originality take center stage. If *Hollywood Shuffle* had never been made, neither would the work of Jamie Foxx, Jim Carrey, or any of the rest of the Wayans family. Without the collaboration of these two trailblazers, we would be living in an alternate reality that would be 75 percent less funny and 100 percent less inspiring.

Wayans and Townsend were originals pioneering a new niche of entertainment. But Adam and Eve were originals in an even truer sense as the original human beings.

Before the fall and temptation of humanity, there was a beautiful level of ignorance. Adam and his wife were naked and unashamed, unaware of the enemy's devices and the evil they would later succumb to. They were who God created them to be: Original beings with no need to cover themselves or hide who they were. Like these first humans, every one of us possesses incredible originality. We are each a one-of-a-kind creation.

YOUR FULL, ONE-OF-A-KIND SELF

The most unique trait of the most unique person you know is an expression of God. Since we were made in God's image and likeness, we all share parts of the totality of God. We take interest in things that God created. Any wholesome interest in life comes from some part of God's heart. Let's remember that God created out of nothing and without a blueprint. He founded time and authored existence. He simply predated what was to come because he always was.

Being original means stepping out into the unfamiliar. It means conquering the unknown. Therefore, using your originality makes you a leader. You are a pioneer, a thought leader, and a trailblazer. Sometimes that is a lonely place to be. In the words of Dr. Myles Munroe, "When you have a purpose and a passion, you must act on it, even if you're the only one who believes in it at the time."[8] You may have people around you. But to be you authentically and unapologetically, you have to walk it alone. When you are lonely and soaring high above what is already present, don't seek comradery in low, or familiar, places. Don't take it to heart when people don't understand you or your work. Endure the awkwardness and misunderstandings and sometimes offense of people's opinions about you. Embrace the unfamiliar and the unknown. Remember that originators don't have a model to follow. And by the time mass production of your ideas comes to pass, you may be off the scene.

If you are to make a mark that can't be traced or photocopied, you have to make new footprints. When making abstract marks, I often put pen or charcoal to paper and just let my hand guide my eyes. It is nearly impossible to duplicate an abstract path. While the abstract may start off as an uncertainty, it eventually becomes something beautiful and one of a kind.

It takes boldness to go where no man or woman has gone before. Newfound territories don't have paved roads. Being original means not worrying about what others may think or do. It's knowing that the direction for you has been chosen but the path has yet to be made smooth. Originality often takes time to be accepted as normal.

To innovate is to make changes in something already established. Innovation introduces new methods, ideas, and outcomes. Creativity is a childlike ability to see things as they are not. Original creativity is seeing things that don't yet exist.

Show up in your artistry as your full self. No one else brings your unique perspective. Your experience and frame of reference are necessary elements for your originality and creativity.

RESPONSE

Take a moment to reflect on what makes you *you*. How did God make you an original, and how does that affect your art? Journal your thoughts.

LIFTED SCRIBBLE

These posters are composite pieces made up of portraits, architecture, patterns, paint strokes, handmade ink strokes, jewels, metals, flowers, and animal prints. The clothing is also tweaked to contain an array of vivid colors. In most of my pieces I turn the skin into black and white. This brings about a reverence for the skin. In this uniformity, Black skin is celebrated as beautiful.

Though the color is stripped, its beauty shines through. It is symbolic of Black people being represented not with a single identity but rather a diverse range of identity. The variety of color signifies the originality of Black people.

6

Taste

I once saw an episode of *Modern Marvels* about how ice cream is made. The episode profiled John Harrison, the official taste tester of Dreyer's Grand Ice Cream. John's tongue is so sensitive that it was insured for one million dollars. He is so excellent in his approach to tasting that he uses a gold-plated spoon to prevent an aftertaste from his utensil. In his approach to critique, John says he looks for three things: an appetizing look, a balanced flavor, and body and texture. His ultimate job is to ensure the quality of the company's product.[9] Just as John developed a valuable, detail-oriented, and experienced taste, we also have to develop taste in our field to be good at determining value. Having such taste develops not only our ability to create but also our ability to critique.

EXPERIENCES SHAPE TASTE

Creative people are aware of every little detail in their surroundings. Having taste is the ability to compare things based on what you've been exposed to. Your frame of reference is determined by your culture, upbringing, training, and the established norm.

Who determines beauty in art? What makes something more desirable than something else? Perhaps it's the hours spent, the artist's intention, or who created the work. To me, it depends on the perception of the audience—the people who experience it. Those who curate a piece of art determine its value. Curators are the key holders to the art world.

Beauty and balance are subjective. We all have our own sense of what is satisfying to the eye and often gravitate toward beauty we've already been exposed to. What's more, when and how we are exposed to something matters. For instance, if moving to a beach or waterfront was a time of great tragedy in someone's life, it may be cause for repulsion or disgust. But if someone encounters a beach destination early in life during a fond time, such as a family vacation, they are more likely to associate that experience with beauty and pleasure.

When I say we all have a sense of what is beautiful, I mean that most people can see the beauty of a sunny spring day and admire God's handiwork. Unless, that is, they have a phobia of things in nature. So, I've come to the conclusion that beauty is subjective. Taste depends on what we've been exposed to. However, we have a responsibility to learn what works well and what other people think works well for them.

As a creative person, you must find the friction between visual satisfaction and exploration. Your work should innovate new ideas while also paying tribute to the past. It can be an old style with new elements. Show respect, but challenge the status quo. Find a healthy balance. Like a new or catchy song, balance composition should seem familiar yet groundbreaking. Cover the song and make it your own. Satisfy with familiarity, but at the same time, make it fresh and new. It should make you want to replay it over and over again.

When it comes to being creative, you have to train your eye. Know what works and what doesn't work, and learn by doing. Experiences

shape your expectations and pique your interest. Rather than play peekaboo with what interests you, regularly expose yourself to what you'd like to do. Interest turns into exploration, which turns into practice. Consistency in practice develops into confidence. And confidence turns into mastery.

RESPONSE

Go have a fresh new experience today. Does that experience match your tastes or broaden them?

HAVE FUN

7
Balance

I ONCE CAME ACROSS a video of a man who was brought to tears as for the first time, he overlooked hills of fall leaves turning color. In 2024, Virginia partnered with an innovative company named EnChroma to become the first state to install colorblind viewfinders at each of its state parks.[10] This initiative enables individuals with colorblindness to see and experience the beauty of nature in a way that is deeply moving. If you have ever sat down in a park on a mild spring day, felt the embrace of a warm summer night breeze, seen beautiful snow-laden trees along a path, or admired a landscape with multicolored leaves, you have experienced the beauty of God's intentional masterpiece.

The journey through the cycle of a year is a purposeful, guided experience. The Lord has balanced the seasons with incredible detail, providing unique beauty for different climates. The shifting colors, weather, and wildlife provide us with artful variety throughout the year. We can learn from divine balance as we apply balance to our art.

BALANCE IS SOMETHING WE LEARN

I don't subscribe to the validity of the golden ratio, but I believe most people have a God-given sense of balance in what they see. If creativity were a recipe, it would need originality, technique, and a knowledgeable sense of what already exists. It would need imagination as well as execution.

In visual art, balance is a dance between composition and color. It considers the ratio of positive and negative space. For instance, if the color is intense the composition needs space to breathe. Learning balance is a rewarding skill. It is the gift that keeps on giving. You can learn to attune your eyes to what works well.

Maybe the need is to flood the space with composition and color, leaving no stone unturned. That may mean putting it all out there by captivating the eye and demanding a thorough gaze from the viewer. Either way, you decide what is appropriate for the space. Some things call for symmetry. Some call for a standard justified composition. Others need the rule of thirds to really balance out the space. You can only know by becoming familiar with how to determine balance. Not only is balance a creative discipline, but it is also the art of soothing the eye rather than agitating it—unless, of course, that's what you're going for.

Abstract art should lend itself to balance as well. Abstract art is not necessarily organized chaos; rather, it is the designated organization of that which no longer makes it chaos. It is the color and balance of positive space and negative space that is pleasing to the eye. Whether in a frame or on a canvas, the space that has been designated to hold this artistic work conveys peace and calm on the outside while a party is going on inside. Balance makes the composition what it is. The environment matters. If I take a Conté crayon and make a mark on a wall, it may not be regarded as art. But if I take that same Conté crayon, place marks on a piece of canvas paper, and then frame it and hang it on a wall, I have just created art.

A piece of art that resonates well with those who experience it often feels familiar to the audience, even while it maintains its originality. It is balanced and makes sense compositionally. Staring at it feels familiar and yet still sparks curiosity. It leaves other artists asking, "Why didn't I think of that?" I slowly observe a piece that I really want to remember, making sure I absorb every detail and placing it into my mental rolodex. I take it in like a gourmet meal a person enjoys once a year, savoring it with my eyes. This idea of balance applies in different ways to music, film, and all kinds of art. A well-balanced piece makes for a better experience for the audience.

PROBLEM SOLVING

Balance serves as a parameter of good creativity. When thinking about balance, consider the medium you're designing in. If you're creating a decal for a car, know that the car is part of the composition. That's why mockups are important. No client wants to see a design without the context of what the final product will look like. To be able to see your design in the intended environment is more than valuable. Consider what surface your art or design is going to be on. How big will it be? What are the necessary elements to make it work for that specific use? How can you tailor the design for the specific need?

Creative problem solving entails finding a way to make things work. In tailoring your creativity to meet the needs of your clients and the project, you are expressing your clients' desires in an artistic manner.

Your skill set must be balanced as well for maximum effectiveness. You can be inspired by the balance in God's creation as you balance your creative projects.

RESPONSE

Try tweaking one of your creative pieces to improve its balance. What do you need more of? What do you need less of?

Young Gifted And Black

8 GROWTH

YOU ONLY GROW AT THE RATE at which you try new things. Creativity needs space to develop. While getting out my children's clothes for the day, I would ask my wife, "What happened to the shirt with the unicorn and ice cream cone on it?" Her reply would be something like, "I gave it away last year because she grew out of it." Sentimental and in disbelief, I would usually repeat what she said in the form of a question. I've realized that my children are growing at an alarming rate. It seems like I was just holding them in my arms without them being able to hold their own head up.

Like children, healthy creativity grows over time. And when creative people look back, they can often be surprised by how much their creativity has grown.

STAGES OF LIFE

God says several times in Genesis to "be fruitful" (Genesis 26:22, 41:52) and in most instances to "be fruitful and multiply" (Genesis 1:22, 28; 8:17; 9:1; 35:11). He tasked humanity with growing the human population on earth. Billions upon billions of people have progressed from childhood to adulthood and beyond, a process that has several distinct phases.

Everyone learns to navigate the phases of life as they come—it's a natural part of growing and maturing. All phases of life offer a unique perspective in regard to creativity. Children have the imagination to see anything as something different. Just give a child a box and see what they can do with it. Their imagination makes them believe anything is possible. Anything in their hands can become new. Teens have tunnel vision when it comes to the things that matter to them. During this stage, they develop a passion for what they create and the journey that it will take them on. They learn to base their identity on being actively creative. This is a pivotal time when their passions are being defined and their creative impulse comes alive.

Young adults have the benefit of knowing what's new and innovative. To know what is "in" is a gift. Adults have developed a stride by gaining experience and being in the industry. Creative practice becomes second nature to them. Older people have the privilege of seeing a lot (and having the coffee mugs and T-shirts to prove it). They can reference their own life to know when something is coming back around. Maturity brings about an enlightening perspective.

We are all amateurs the first time we face something and later become experts through our memories and life experiences. Creative phases are no different. Artistic growth is a journey of exploration. There's always something to discover and new methods to explore. Just when we think we have become a pro, something new comes up, making us start from square one in a particular arena. We are all on a journey of growth through life's many phases, with bumps in the road and unexpected twists and turns to navigate in real time. I'm encouraging us to look around as we journey. Remember the details. Welcome the beauty of not knowing everything at once.

If we are fortunate enough on our journey of artistic growth, we will arrive upon moments of self-discovery. When learning new methods and disciplines, and faced with the possibility of inadequacy, I discovered that I had more skills than I didn't have. And what I didn't have, I could learn. As I matured, I discovered that not only am I artistic, but I am also an artist. Every experience I've had, every creative discipline that I've been fortunate enough to develop, has left a mark on the gears of my creative mind. It has all molded me into an artist. The things I *had* to do prepared me for the projects I *wanted* to do. As Paul said, "Necessity is laid upon me"(1 Corinthians 9:16 KJV). In the past when I didn't create, I felt like I was missing out on something. Now, when I don't create, I feel like the world is missing out on something.

OIL THOSE GEARS

Just as children don't grow up overnight, our creativity cannot mature in a day. Growth takes time. Our generation is used to fast resolutions to everything, but patience is still a virtue.

Creativity is like a muscle. If you don't keep it active, it will deteriorate. It's not exactly like riding a bike. Just like the adage suggests, "If you don't use it, you lose it." Creativity is a gear that steadily turns. The more you use it, the more oiled it gets. Dr. Maya Angelou said, "You can't use up creativity. The more you use, the more you have."[11] In other words, when you continually use your creativity, it can't help but grow. You have to challenge yourself. Creativity translates well. If you are a creative person, you have the proclivity to be trustworthy in identifying that *it* factor. Welcome opportunities to grow, don't run from them. It is the chance to come up with a winning idea. If you have the ingredients, you'll come out with a delicious recipe.

Keep growing your creativity by staying sharp. If a dry season for work is coming your way, make your own work. Do your own projects. Maintain your skill set until things pick back up. If no one is calling you, call someone else to create your own project. Just like in the medical field, there is always a training or new certification to obtain. To maintain something is to help it to grow. Most musical instruments require maintenance. You can't store them away and expect the same sound as before. In most cases, the instrument at least has to be tuned. In the same way, we must keep using our skills if we want to stay sharp and keep growing.

Maintaining your growth may involve partnering with someone who knows how to get things done in the current climate, someone who understands contemporary methods while you come up with the concepts. Their acumen and credibility may serve as a vehicle for your knowledge and experience. Team up to grow together.

RESPONSE

Take a moment to reflect on your journey with creativity. How have you matured as an artist? Write down some thoughts in a journal. Then challenge your self to venture out. Use your creativity in another area that you've had an interest in but never tried.

START NOW

9 CONFIDENCE

CREATIVE PEOPLE CAN LEARN a lot from small children. Kids don't put the brakes on life until they learn better. They go all in. They have unparalleled confidence—until we tell them "Don't do that" or "Don't say that." You must develop confidence for your gift to be effective. A year ago, I was not comfortable doing the things I'm doing now. Five years ago, what I do now was nowhere on my radar. Creative confidence comes with experience.

I did a photo shoot once with a spoken word poet. I had never done anything like this before, and it was not going well. An experienced photographer is meant to help the subject feel calm, but I didn't have much experience posing subjects. Just as my confidence was faltering, my wife suggested I have the poet perform a poem. It worked! Not only did it give me pure gold for the photos, but it also made my subject relax and act natural. After that, my confidence with photo shoots rose significantly.

LIONS, GIANTS, AND BEARS

When we are introduced to David, he is tending to his father's sheep. Though his lineage is briefly mentioned in the book of Ruth, 1 Samuel 16 is where we are formally introduced to him. If it were up to his father, Jesse, one of his seven other sons would have been anointed king. But David wasn't found among them; he was in the field. David was a multifaceted creative person and so much more. He was a poet, composer, musician, shepherd, warrior, and king—undoubtedly the most celebrated psalmist of biblical times. Though he was a polymath of sorts, he is most widely known for slaying Goliath.

The reach of this story goes far beyond religious circles. In sports when an underdog wins against what seems like an undefeatable foe, it is deemed as a David and Goliath matchup. When confronted with the possibility of facing Goliath, David seemed to be unimpressed and unintimidated. His heart did not fail because of the giant. Why was this the case? The passage does not say that the Spirit of the Lord was upon David at that moment. What prepared him?

Goliath asked that a man be chosen to fight him. But David volunteered himself and rose to the challenge. He had confidence because he had experience: while tending to his father's sheep, he had encountered a lion and a bear. David's confidence in God and comfort by his experience left him with this attitude: "The Lord who rescued me from the paw of the lion and the paw of the bear will rescue me from the hand of this Philistine" (1 Samuel 17:37). Not only did he win, but he also claimed the prize that Saul promised. Defeating the giant was David's defining moment.

What is your giant? What is the thing that you want to define you? If you can have the confidence that comes from experience, you too can slay lions, giants, and bears on your creative journey.

CONFIDENT CREATIVITY

To build confidence we have to ask ourselves, *What am I creating*? Ideas are great, and most things start with them, but to bring our art into existence, we must move past concepts and flesh out our ideas. Hypothetical creativity stagnates confidence, while confident creativity takes the necessary steps to make the idea a reality, even when that reality isn't perfect.

Often, our confidence falters because we are afraid of other people seeing our work. But we have to create even when we are not sharing our work. There are times we should share our work with the world, but sharing publicly should not determine whether or not we create. Sometimes just sitting back and taking in the art we have produced is enough of a confidence boost to share our work with others.

CONSTRUCTING CONFIDENCE

If mature creativity is a building, you must take several steps to get it up to code. Project completion is necessary to build creative confidence. Small projects, as well as free projects, are your friend. To cultivate your skills, find someone who can't pay you but will benefit from your services. It may be a church, an aspiring model, or a nonprofit. There is nothing wrong with being transactional with the right motive. Find someone or something whose values you identify with and that you would like to reinforce. In exchange for your services, you get to share what you helped them accomplish. You need to build a well-rounded portfolio. I decided to become a mentor because when I went back to school as an adult, I found that the younger people in the program had great skills without much real-world application. Some people have expertise without a college degree, and some people have the degree without any of the experience. It takes both credentials and credibility to be successful and build confidence.

Sometimes you have to work for little or nothing until you can demand what your work is worth. Know that your work will get there if you put in the time and effort to develop your skills. Get some projects under your belt to see how quick on your feet you are in real-world applications. Projects don't often come knocking at your door or into your inbox until you have a track record. Until that time comes, go find them. Ask an entrepreneur, a small business, or a budding social media influencer if you can work on a project for them. If they don't have anything in mind, pitch them a worthwhile idea. Show the value of your creativity and how it could be beneficial to them. When you're done, show it to the world—*your* world, that is. That includes your family, your church, your neighbors, and your friends. Keeping the incredible things that you do to yourself helps no one and will get you nowhere. So take to social media like it is a mountaintop. Tell family members at holiday gatherings. Post a flier at church or at the local coffee shop. Partner with a school that has no budget for creative projects. Get in where you fit in. I didn't always have consistent clients, but I never stopped creating. If I had waited for consistent solicited projects, my creativity would have dried up. I endeavored to keep it oiled in order to keep it alive.

Be aspirational. Know that you have every right to show up and be your full creative self. Know that you don't have to ask permission to create. If what you tried doesn't work out, your attempt was not wasted. Instead, recognize that unused ideas are the biggest waste. You choke the life out of inspiration when you ignore it. Your creative impulse should not be timid or apprehensive. Rather, it should give itself license to exist. It must carve out space to be free and unashamed.

RESPONSE

Tell someone about one of your creations today. Let them see your artwork, listen to your music, read your poem, or experience whatever else you have made. You can be confident that your art is worth it.

AND WE WILL SEE WHAT WILL BECOME OF HIS DREAMS.

CREATE INTENTIONAL OUTCOMES

10 Intention

No other creative work is as emotion-evoking as cinema. I remember when I first took full notice of *Do the Right Thing*.[12] I had never experienced storytelling in that way before. The music, the color palate, the bold camera angles—it was all so Brooklyn you could taste it, so immersive you could feel the heat from the TV screen. I can only imagine the euphoria and agitation that theater-goers must have felt when it was first released. Spike Lee took us all on an emotional roller coaster as the heat and racial tensions rose on this condensed and diverse block of Bed-Stuy. Even at a young age, I realized this was unique storytelling. Lee dubs his films "Joints" and is known for quite a few trademarks in his films, one of the most recognizable being his signature double dolly shot. It involves two platforms on which the actor and camera are pulled on a track. The floating shot symbolizes surreal moments and, oftentimes, characters moving toward an inescapable fate. Lee is intentional in connecting the subject matter through his unique perspective. When you watch a Spike Lee Joint, it feels like you are viewing an experience that can only be delivered by him.

What story are you trying to tell with your art? What idea are you trying to convey? What emotion do you want to evoke? What questions are you trying to ask? In other words, what is your intention for your creativity? Be purposeful about the impact you want your art to have.

GOD'S INTENTIONS

We were created in the image of God, but in essence, we were a new creation. At a point outside of time, God determined our existence within time and crafted us in his image and in his likeness (Genesis 1:26), reflecting his purposeful intent in the process of our creation. He was and is intentional.

In creation, God saw the nonexistent and brought it into existence in perfectly calculated order. He was deliberate in what and how he created, from humankind to animals to vegetation. Because we are made in his image, we should also be intentional about what and how we create. Mastering the creative process means being obsessed with the details.

Every intricate part deserves our full attention. As we read the Scriptures, we find that God is a creative—the best one indeed. No one creates better than he does. He is intentional and attentive to his creation. The ultimate multi-tasker, he is in all and knows all. While holding together the fabric and order of the universe, he pays attention to the smallest details in our lives. After all, even the hairs on our heads are numbered (Luke 12:7). He is concerned about the slightest features, like a sculptor carefully molding a clay model. Not only did he create us, but he also has plans for our lives. Just as God has a purpose for all that he creates, so should we.

PLANNING WITH INTENTIONALITY

It is important to be purposeful about the experience we want our intended audience to have when we create. Guiding our audience's emotions and appealing to their senses require careful consideration. We ask ourselves, *What journey do we want our audience to embark on?* In abstract visual art, the presentation is open-ended, and although everyone is presented with the same elements, each viewer is left to arrive at their own conclusion. Still, when we are intentional from start to finish, we can guide some of the viewer's experience.

Intentional creation takes detail, thought, and purpose. Planning is key to carrying out creative ideas. We have to schedule time and dedicate physical space to create. Be intentional about making sure that space speaks to you and inspires you to be creative. You are an artist. Take ownership of that. Wear clothes that inspire you to create when you look in the mirror. Control the environment around you. Go places that stimulate your mind. Sometimes it takes finding the right atmosphere to be productive. And if you can't find it, make it. Design a life that inspires you. Find ways to excite your mind. After all, it is your main tool.

Everything you create is filtered through your thought process, which is influenced by your surroundings. It could mean going the long way home to stir up the right emotions. What fosters imagination in your mind? Know yourself and know what triggers your artistry. If you don't know, find out. Be intentional about living in a way that makes being inspired to create easy and, above all, normal. Your creative life should not live in a dusty box in your closet. If it does, dust it off. Decorate your walls with it. Pin it to your refrigerator or make it the wallpaper on your phone. Be in a head space where inspiration can happen at any moment.

When my space is cluttered, I find it difficult to create. I have a list of things I need in order to avoid getting distracted, such as wide-open space and windows that give natural light. I am intentional about having a set space in my home to create. Some would call it a sacred space, while others would call it a man cave. I call it a studio. Labeling is up to you; it's part of being deliberate in your approach to your creativity. You have the power to be purposeful. Intentionality goes beyond creative practice—it is a major part of the creative process.

RESPONSE

Make a plan. Be intentional about the details of a project or series of projects. Let the power of your intention shine through your work. Don't forget to be obsessed with the details. Write them out and make them plain directives.

CREATION TAKES DETAIL, THOUGHT AND PURPOSE.

11 FOCUS

What would it look like if you approach your creative gift as more than just a hobby? What if it is a means of communication and expression, a language that helps to interpret whatever you are experiencing? It would become a constant in your life, not only when you are bored or need to pass time, but as a record of your experiences. It would mean creating in both celebration and defeat, creating just because and for just cause. Creation, in this manner, is liberated thought. If creativity is to take such a vital role in our lives, it will require incredible focus.

My creativity moves a million miles a minute. It is a freeway of thought, pondering, and inspiration. I have to be intentional about focus due to my creative brain. My creativity, at times, is like an HBCU drum major high-stepping while playing an accordion and beatboxing. The proclivity to act on some other idea that I'm inspired to do is ever present.

I'm easily inspired to create, but my creative practice always has to catch up with my thought process. The only way to do so is to single out ideas and put them into motion. I find it helpful to write my ideas down and take screenshots. I keep little composition notebooks around the house that I call idea books. A moment of inspiration can dwindle and yield nothing if I don't document it for future reference. So I have to cut out distractions like phone notifications and social media. But at other times, putting on an old movie or WrestleMania episode that I'm familiar with keeps me focused by subduing the two-way street that is my brain.

STIR IT UP

Focusing on what you want to do—when you want to do it—and how you can get it done keeps you from getting stuck in hypothetical thought. It puts things in motion.

For me, creative focus has been a means of coping with the stress of a stacked project workload. When I feel overwhelmed, focusing on what is in front of me helps me not to feel as though the other tasks I have are an ever-present cloud looming over me. Many people fail to focus in the moment because of other things that take up real estate in their minds.

Be present in the moment. Of course you're working toward an end result, but be *here* now. Be fully engaged in the process. Giving your best effort requires full attention, so be proactive in your approach to focusing.

Just as Paul tells Timothy to stir up the gift in him (2 Timothy 1:6), God's gift has allowed you to create at the level of mastery. However, reaching that point means learning how to focus. It means being present in the moment and putting your best foot forward with clarity and freedom of thought. Block out what is necessary to concentrate. The enemy of focus is distraction.

When I'm creating, having other things going on in the background helps me to focus. For example, I enjoy playing a familiar movie or worship song because I know what to expect. It's like a controlled distraction that keeps me aware yet focused on my creative process. However, this rarely ever happens when I'm watching something new, as taking in new information involves a lot of effort for me. I value information and take the time to place it in my mental rolodex.

When an idea tries to arrest your attention in the middle of a creative session, document it so that you can revisit and implement it. If it's something in your immediate power to do, take action as swiftly as you can. If it will take time, collaboration, or untapped resources, be as detailed as you can while the inspiration is freshest in your mind. You can't afford to lose any details to time and hesitation. So if that means recording a voice memo, writing notes in a notepad, or taking digital notes that you can access from anywhere, document your ideas at the moment of inspiration. Then get back to what you were working on and stay focused.

RESPONSE

Take one project and work on it every day for one week. If possible, put your other projects on hold until this one comes alive. Focus in on this particular task with the utmost attentiveness. Listen to one of these playlists while doing so.

show up

12 Rest

An unexpected nap is a gift to the body. A planned nap feels like a stop at the gas station during a long road trip; it can leave you refreshed and ready to tackle the rest of your day. I'm well acquainted with road trips, whether it's a sixteen-hour journey to Mississippi from Gary, Indiana, or reluctantly navigating the mountains of Pennsylvania to get to New England. If you travel with a group of people, half the fun of the journey is getting there. It's going to the rest stops and seeing the landmarks and attractions that you can only experience on the way.

Just like people on road trips, artists need to stop and rest. I'm intentional about rest. When I'm going on a retreat or vacation, I go off the grid. I don't bring a camera or a laptop. It is tempting to grab my phone and take to social media when traveling to a new place because today's logic is that if it didn't happen on social media, it didn't happen at all. But as conflicting as it is, I always remind myself that I didn't make the trip to document it or share it. I came to rest.

Sabbath Rest

It's important to note that God implemented rest as an active part of his creative process. Unlike God, we as human beings have limitations.

Artistic creation takes a lot out of us. We have to ask ourselves, *Why would an all-powerful God who never sleeps implement rest in his creative process?* This shows us two things, the first being the importance of a sabbath. Not only does God model the sabbath for us in his process of creation, but he also commands it of us in Exodus 20:8. Remembering the Sabbath day is more than taking a restful pause. It is a time set apart for God, not only in our weekly routine but whenever we need it. It is a time of reflection, rest, and worship. God's modeling of the Sabbath shows us that creation is worthy of celebration and reflection. For us, this means rest is beneficial for our spiritual, mental, and physical health. If the Creator of the universe took time to rest and admire his creation, we as his creation must learn that the creation-and-rest cycle is necessary for healthy creativity. God created, rested, and celebrated. The reflection comes in the examination of what he made: "Then God looked over all he had made, and he saw that it was very good!" (Genesis 1:31 NLT).

Throughout the whole process of creation, we see a pattern of God speaking to set things in order. When he speaks, the void transforms into whatever he intends it to be. After the period of him speaking, something changes. Notice the pattern in Genesis 1: he said, he set, he formed, he saw that it was good, he celebrated the quality of his work, then he finally rested. God not only modeled this pattern for us, but he also insisted on it when rolling out the standards of living in the Ten Commandments. Rest and relaxation are needed for the rhythms of the creative mind. What we can take away from this example is a balance between planning, labor, reflection, celebration, and rest.

God spoke everything into existence, provided the materials, and then made us from those materials. He divided the waters. He came into the studio of earth and turned the lights on. He got ready to

REST

work and started the clock of time. After he was done, he sat back, rested, and said that it was good. Reflecting on the quality of his work, he saw that it was worth the effort and the planning. God, who is ageless and sovereign; God, who is ancient of days; God, who is omnipresent and omnipotent; God, who has all power and ability and was so diligent, passionate, and active in his creative process, took the time to rest at the end.

RECHARGE YOUR ARTISTRY

After you've toiled over a project for a long time, it can be hard to get out of that headspace. But after you've rested and revisited it, you can look at it with clear eyes. You can see it for what it really is—either a gem of accomplishment or something that needs improvement. It is necessary for creative people to go a certain period of time without creating in order to reset and have fresh focus.

In an age of constant contact, it is necessary for us to step away from it all sometimes. The mind was not made to keep up with the twenty-four-hour news cycle or to keep tabs on every aspect of your life. All that information at your fingertips in one place at one time can be pretty stressful. The filing cabinet of the brain is meant to compartmentalize and keep certain things in different folders. Too much time on social media takes all the folders from the drawers, dumps them on a messy table, and forces you to find them randomly as best as you can. Structured time to rest and retreat from screens is one of the best ways to reorganize those mental drawers.

Remember that God stepped out of eternity, created time and seasons, and ordained a practice of rest for his children. As a person with a creative impulse, you may find it difficult to rest your mind until you've accomplished what you have imagined. It's hard to turn the gears of creativity off. But rest recharges you. Resting and restarting keeps creativity flowing as it should.

RESPONSE

Take thirty minutes today to do something restful. Take a nap, go for a walk in nature, spend time with loved ones—anything that rejuvenates you.

13 RHYTHM

THIS WORLD THAT GOD CREATED is not stagnant, nor is it monotonous. Creation moves in fascinating rhythms. As a part of its life cycle, a plant dies but always comes back more vibrant. God allows life in plants to be suspended in a way that also preserves them. The cycle of floral life should inspire us as creative people to know that things come back around. Seasons do change. Art has the ability to transform dilapidated spaces that are in need of new life.

God has established rhythms in nature, and people can emulate him by creating rhythms in their own lives. Consider the training of athletes. The hardest part is practice, the discipline of getting in condition. They work to be in peak condition at the time of competition. In the one-hundred-meter race, an Olympic sprinter works four years to run a race in under ten seconds. A basketball player puts up hundreds if not thousands of shots a week to develop enough of a rhythm to be lethal from his chosen spot on the court. All this athletic training represents life rhythms that athletes use to maximize their performance.

Artists can utilize this concept of rhythms to optimize their artistic skill. People tend to associate artistry with spur-of-the-moment inspiration, and there is some truth to that, but intentional life rhythms are even more important for creative people than spontaneity. Consistent creative practice gets your skills and your mind in tiptop shape to perform.

SOLO TIME

One of the most important aspects of our life rhythms is creating time for solitude. As creative people, we have to manage our alone time well. It's important to take the time to perfect our craft. If we are fortunate enough to have quiet time, we can't afford to waste it. And if we don't have time for solitude, we have to create some. Achieving excellence sometimes means late nights and early mornings. Borrow some time from social media. While social media can inspire, it can also stir up feelings of sadness and take our quiet time prisoner. We must master our alone time to ensure our creative practice stays healthy. Doing so means protecting our quiet time and remembering that when we participate in creative practice, not all our spare time is for leisure; rather, a portion of it is for creating. Just like God stepped out onto nothing to bring forth the universe and our existence as we know it, there is something sacred about creating in a place of quiet and solitude, a place in which we are undisturbed. In these times I have discovered more about myself and found creative breakthrough.

Sometimes happiness can be a place. We often create better under the right circumstances, and creation can serve as a means of escape. I engage in what I call the "crea-cation" challenge, in which I take a vacation or staycation to create. Sometimes the quality of our creative work reflects the quality of everything else in our lives, and we just need a vacation. My happy place is near water, especially water that requires a flight to reach it. But that's just me. The destination is less important than your intention for this time. I invite you to engage in this challenge too. Be it local or abroad, physically get to a place that inspires you. Document how you feel. Does inspiration flow more freely? Are you distracted by your new and unfamiliar surroundings? Is this something worth continuing or not? Do something, go somewhere, and see something new, but be consistent in your creative practice. Then see the gold that you create.

RESPONSE

I challenge all visual artists to set aside time to build a rhythm. To activate our creative rhythm, we have to stretch ourselves. A thirty-day challenge is a perfect opportunity to put this into action. There are many similar challenges to boost creativity, all with various requirements and recommendations, but I suggest this simple challenge as a part of going through this book.

There are two ways I would recommend going about this. One way is to create a standalone piece every day for thirty days. For designers and digital artists, that may mean producing a poster. For painters, that may mean creating a new painting every day. For musicians, this may mean a new song. Filmmakers might write a new scene every day. Culinary artists might cook a new dish inspired by a new region of the world. The second way I would recommend attempting this thirty-day challenge is to create a new piece every day as part of a larger series. This is not just beneficial to visual artists—I recommend this as a discipline-developing tool for any creative person. Series are so effective because they are based on a well-developed formula. Just as we appreciate marathon watching episodes of our favorite series, the intrigue is in how the theme will be closely aligned but different among the parts of the series, while the outcome is always in the realm of the story's arc. This exercise will engage our creative mind, serving as a boot camp to whip it into shape. Some of our superpowers have not been unlocked because we haven't had to function in that space enough. We haven't had to think in the trenches of rapid ideation, which involves brainstorming with limited time. This challenge encourages quick thinking and creating, and before we know it, our brains become accustomed to taking advantage of opportunities to create. Whether we choose to create a new standalone work every day or a new piece as part of a series that connects ideas, either method can help us develop a consistent rhythm.

KEEPGOING

14
DISRUPTION

EVEN AFTER FINDING OUR RHYTHM, we can't get too comfortable. Comfort often signals that it's time for a change. I worked as a digital media specialist for a nonprofit organization for over three years. When I was hired in December 2020, I was not expected to be in the office aside from special events, conferences, and photo shoots for magazine articles. For the first two years, I primarily worked remotely from another state. In my last year, I moved to Chicago and was closer to the company office. Post-pandemic, the company required employees within commuting distance to work in the office more frequently. Just when I became comfortable driving in more regularly and I stopped needing to use the GPS to get to work, it was time for me to leave that job. Life and creativity can be like that. Just when you feel as though you've found your rhythm and you get comfortable in your approach to creating, disruption comes. This disruption can be a new method or a new software or device that changes the entire landscape of how things are done.

Creativity has a way of disrupting the conventional. New trends emerge when new methods are developed, mastered, and duplicated and when influential industry leaders recognize the value of something new.

ORGANIZE *chaos*

Take hip-hop, for instance. Though music was its driving force, its impact goes beyond music. It has influenced our fashion, attitudes, mannerisms, slang, broadcasting, and dance, particularly in Western society. No one can deny that American culture has been shaped by hip-hop and street culture in the last fifty years, and it all extends from this art form that spread like a disruptive wildfire. Whether you listen to hip-hop music or not, it has undeniably been one of the most influential cultural phenomena of the last fifty years. Initially not accepted in mainstream culture, it has now become a huge part of the mainstream. Creative disruption challenges the conventional and can transform the status quo.

When I was growing up, my mother would often call my brothers and cousins to rearrange the furniture, often at inconvenient times when we were already doing something else. Though we would get frustrated, we were always amazed at how she could rearrange the same furniture but get a new look every time. What would our creativity look like if we didn't confine ourselves to the same old mode of doing things?

THE POWER OF THE PIVOT

Don't be thrown off by a change in plans. I've experienced so many shifting variables in the form of changes, revisions, and even a flat-out change of concept right before completion. I've been the cause of all of the above as well. But creative people can turn mistakes into innovation. However, the power of the pivot is not just the ability to redirect a project; it is the instinct to redirect creative methods and skill sets. I started off as a designer and saw a need for photography. After I learned photography, I garnered rhythm in mixed media art. That passion then turned to video. Pivoting is leveraging the avenues in which you create. It is evolving your passions to the next logical step in your creative journey. It is turning disruption into opportunity. Creative chops can be transferred to different methods and skill sets. You are the greatest asset for your own creativity. As long as you are in the driver's seat, you will find success in whatever iteration of creativity you choose to function in.

What would it look like if our familiar places were rearranged periodically? When things get stagnant, or even when they are going well or when you become too comfortable, it's important to move the furniture around and shake things up. Rearranging established elements can create a new look and inspire creativity. Sometimes creating in a different location may spark new ideas. So get out and explore the world while creating; it may just be the disruption you need.

RESPONSE

Have you experienced a disruption today or this week? Try turning it into a moment for creativity.

ABSTRACT INK STROKES

These started as ink strokes in a notepad. From there, I took photos of them with my phone and placed them in Adobe Illustrator.

15

Creating Through Pain

In 1932, after the tragic loss of his wife, Nette, during childbirth and his infant son a day later, Thomas A. Dorsey sat down at his piano—confused, frustrated and out of options—and penned,

> Precious Lord, take my hand,
> lead me on, let me stand;
> I am tired, I am weak, I am worn.[13]

Hence, modern gospel music was born. Dorsey did something unique in that he merged the subject matter of blues and the religious nature and hymn format of gospel music. Though this song and many of his other creations around this time were controversial, he would go on to be known as the father of gospel music.

Dorsey allowed beauty to flow out of his pain. His hardship was an inspiration for his creativity. The music didn't make his loss any less devastating, but it provided him an avenue for healing, and it blessed innumerable people in the process.

Creativity is a gift from God, especially in painful circumstances. Genesis 16 tells the story of Hagar, the enslaved Egyptian woman who

Sarai gave to her husband, Abram, as a surrogate mother for the son God promised them. Imagine Hagar's pain when Sarai, the one who set this whole plan in motion, grew jealous when her servant became a mother. Hagar's pregnancy also caused Hagar to resent Sarai. After being mistreated by Sarai, Hagar in her distress fled into the desert, where God appeared to her. She called the Creator "the God who sees me" (Genesis 16:13). Hagar's name for God poured out from her heart's creative expression and gave language to their intimate encounter. This is the first time that God, the Creator, is referred to in Scripture creatively as a part of individual intimate expression. God saw Hagar for who she was and met her in her pain.

God sees us for who we are too. He sees our humanity, our ethnicity, and our gender. He sees our individuality, our identity, and our creativity. If we're in the wilderness, he knows why we're there and will meet us where we are. When God meets us, we may pour out our hearts through art, music, writing, and other creative expressions. For example, an encounter with God might spark your creativity to arrange a breathtaking bouquet of colorful flowers. In whatever way you express yourself creatively, an encounter with him warrants a response. Hagar used her pain as inspiration to produce a new name for God.

REFUGE

Why does it seem like the greatest creations come out of the greatest pain? Sometimes, it's necessary to create through discomfort. This is a time when we are incapable of being indifferent or halfhearted. Pain alters our ordinary routine, bringing discomfort that often leaves space in our life for something beautiful to blossom. What could fit in that space if we turned the passion from that pain into something

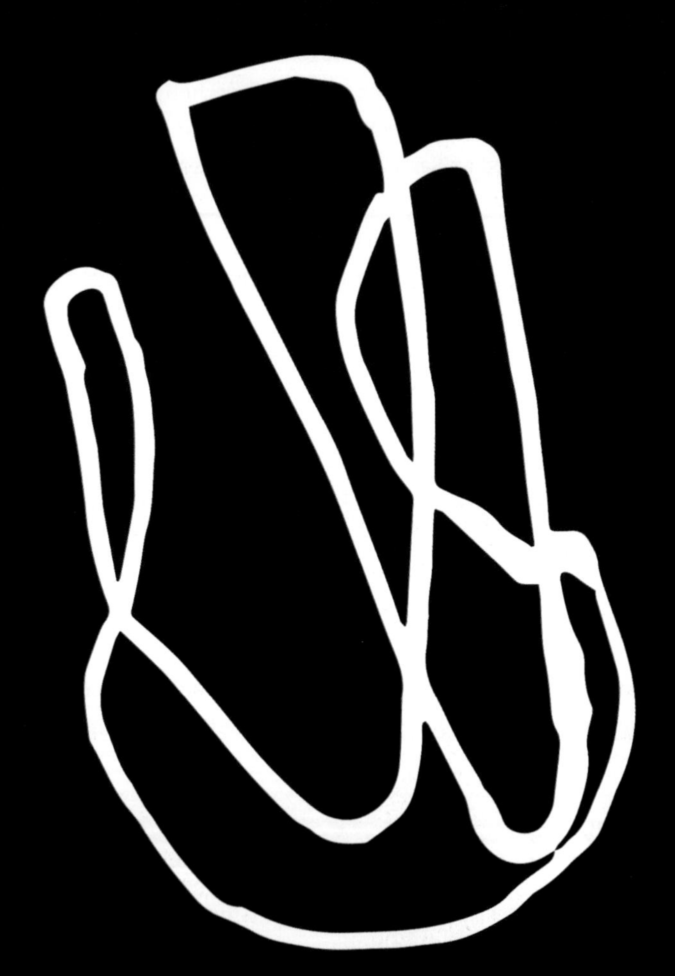

nondestructive? What would it look like if we could direct our strong emotions to a sanctuary? I'm not saying there is a big red button for this. But I am saying that creativity can be a companion of pain—one that won't say the wrong thing or fail to listen. Grief is a fleeting emotion. Just as Natasha Smith suggests in *Can You Just Sit with Me?*, "For sure, grief is hard, and grief hurts. Grief can be heavy and sometimes crippling. Grief can be seen as more of a feeling than an event, more relative than concrete."[14] Let your temporary emotions interact with your creativity. Don't stop in these times of struggle.

Those who are able to maintain a consistent creative practice through the toughest of times often create great things. It is in these moments that creativity becomes a refuge, a rescuing lifeline in the sea of sorrow. If you can manage to harness focused creativity in these times, you will unlock a fount of imagination. I'm not suggesting that you not do what is necessary to address pain and the traumas of life. I'm saying a creative practice can be a means of healing for a creative person. When the things that you can't control are uncontrollable, you have this secret sanity.

At the height of emotion, there is a certain depth you can explore when art is an outlet rather than a hobby. You create a sacred space for something consistent that you can hold onto.

Let creativity be your journal. Use it to celebrate, to explore, to soothe, and to unwind. Let it be an outlet to express the energy and emotion that adversity builds up. Redirect that energy into a safe place. There are a few different ways to do so. You can use it to document your journey and cope in real time with the things you are facing. In visual art, this may mean translating your feelings into a piece of art. Don't waste that energy and emotion. Don't keep it bottled up. Express it in a way that is therapeutic and functional.

Focus in. Block out the urge to stop your creative practice. Some would say this mindset is unhealthy, but it is often in these difficult times that something is triggered in your creativity. Allow your creativity to be a healthy outlet where you can release your emotions. Steal away into a place of fervor in your work. Let your depth of feeling and passion be a guiding force into great creation.

RESPONSE

What painful experiences have affected you? How has creativity been an outlet for your pain and a source of healing? Write about it in your journal.

create when in *pain*

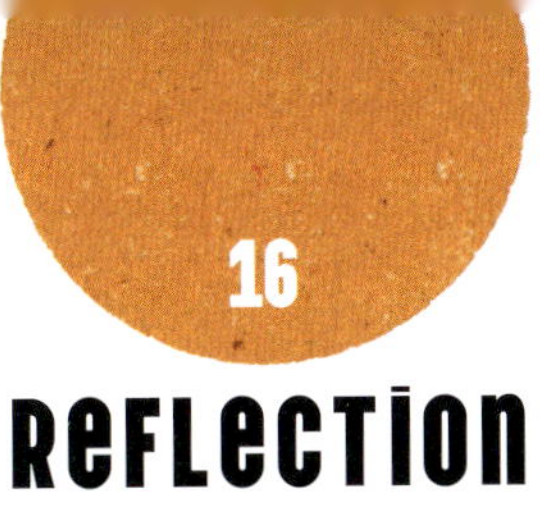

16 Reflection

It fascinates me when I hear of actors who don't watch their own films. We movie fans can't imagine not seeing the movies we love over and over again. But some actors see it from a different perspective. Many of them don't choose to reflect on their work in that way, and certainly not as frequently as a fan might. Denzel Washington told British newspaper *The Times*, "I watch it so I know what I'm talking about. But I haven't watched any film from my past from start to finish, not even *Malcolm X*. All you see is what you did wrong. Also, why would you do it anyway?"[15]

Denzel's question is a provocative one—why bother reflecting? Despite this curious approach by some actors, reflection is a vital part of the creative process. Revisiting old projects is good and necessary. Reflection can gauge growth. While it has the power to embarrass you or empower you, reflection ultimately shows you how you have grown in a tremendous way. Let's consider some of the key benefits of reflection. It gives you the power to go back in time and plan for the future. It is the rearview mirror for what you have already encountered. If you were a boxer and knew you had a rematch with someone who is difficult to fight, wouldn't it be beneficial to go back and watch the previous fight? Reflection is a gift to those who want to improve themselves and their creative practice.

Not all reflection leads to regret and regrouping. After all, in God's creation process, he reflected and saw that all he had made was "very good." He looked back over what he had done and validated it completely.

TAKE INVENTORY

I worked at a suit store for three years. The one time of year we took inventory was always a tedious task for us. I'm sure the store managers felt differently, but I loved it. It was one of the only times of year that the whole store staff came together. Even our regional manager came in to be a part of the process. We'd start after we closed and then go out to eat. While communal reflection was fun in this job, there is a heavy aspect of reflection as well.

Part of reflection is being honest about our track record. We have to take inventory sometimes and reflect on what we have done. Ideas are one thing, but what have we executed on? God has given us abilities, gifts, and intellect. He has anointed us to do specific things. How are we using those gifts?

Find a way to measure what you have done and how you have performed to see what did and didn't work. For content creators, that may mean analyzing numbers and analytics. Develop a portfolio of work. Every creative person should be able to point to samples of their work to showcase what they have done. This way, your practice of reflection can pay dividends in your artistic development.

RESPONSE

Work on developing a portfolio of pieces that you have completed. Pick your very best work and put it on a website or a social media account. For some of you, this means putting something into physical form. If what you produce is not digital, take photos or videos of what you created. Just be sure to make it easily accessible.

17 comparison

In graphic design class, I had to submit a midterm deliverable to present what I had been working on up to that point. The result would be a zine, a small booklet containing original work and text that would be self-published and distributed independently. People could choose to photocopy zines, make each by hand, or simply print them. For this class, we all took over the professor's computer to share our screens on the projector. When it was my turn to share the pieces I had made, I was unveiling a style and method that was new to me.

For this series of works, I took free-use portraits to create composite posters. With the posters I made double exposure images using textures, photos of architecture, animal prints, text, original ink scribbles, vibrant colors, and more. When I shared my work, I received favorable comments that made me feel like a million bucks. But when my professor saw the series, she said, "Oh, this is like Temi Coker."

Who? I thought. After my presentation, I asked my professor for the name of the person she had mentioned. When I searched for Coker's work, I went through the gamut of emotions. I was inspired, I was mad, I was embarrassed, and I was overwhelmed by the beauty of his work. He had not only used this style long before I did, but he had mastered it. Instead of throwing up my hands, I paid attention. Coker's body of work was much larger than mine. I didn't set out to catch up with him right away. Rather, I appreciated his work as inspirational. I took note of how my work was similar in concept but different in method. At that moment, I didn't set out to be the next Temi Coker but to be the best me that I could be.

Like my professor, everyone has the liberty to critique. But you have to be selective in what and who you listen to. If you put work out into the world—whether on social media, a website, or a gallery exhibit—be prepared for solicited and unsolicited criticism. Critique was always a disconcerting part of any art class I took. I'm sure this sentiment was shared with many others who found themselves in this setting. You don't leave a share out feeling indifferent. You are grateful for people's praise of your work but defensive if they misunderstand the ideas and logic of your method. Your work is displayed for all to see, and it all succumbs to the same scrutiny. You leave the circle vulnerable and unable to unhear the slightest tip that someone provided. However, the key is listening with your ears and not your heart.

HEALTHY COMPARISON

Galatians 6:4 (AMP) says, "But each one must carefully scrutinize his own work [examining his actions, attitudes, and behavior], and then he can have the personal satisfaction and inner joy of doing something commendable without comparing himself to another." It's important to note that the Bible is exhorting us against comparison regarding our good works. When it comes to creativity, on the other hand, healthy comparison is essential.

It's important to have a healthy and functional relationship with comparison to foster creative growth. Unhealthy comparison fosters

CREATE
COMPARE
CONTRAST

resentment, jealousy, and contempt. It can impair our creativity. For this reason, some believe that we shouldn't compare ourselves or our work to anyone else, but that's not realistic. We should compare in ways that inspire us, not stifle us. Healthy comparison involves gauging our work against someone else's for the purpose of improvement. This process can also serve as a compass to see if we are going in the right direction. Even if we find that we are different from the person we compare ourself to, this form of healthy comparison can allow our strengths to shine through. Doing so enables us to celebrate the work we've been doing that has paid off.

Comparison should compel us to aim higher in our own efforts. It should never compel us to tear someone else down or disqualify ourselves from future success. Healthy comparison cultivates admiration, inspiration, accountability, and development. It involves finding someone who already occupies the space we want to be in. Having a mentor is a relationship based on comparison. It's gauging where you are now and having an escort guide you to where you want to be. That's why this form of mentoring does not work well with someone who is a peer. Any person who sees themself going beyond their current creative level wants guidance from someone who far exceeds them in tenor or level of mastery. This form of comparison provides a path to our dreams. Their success enables you to dream with purpose and expectation. It is assurance that your dream can one day become a reality. In the words of the Reverend Dr. Martin Luther King Jr., "If you can't fly then run, if you can't run then walk, if you can't walk then crawl, but whatever you do you have to keep moving forward."[16]

Some critiques are just for the sake of expressing disapproval. However, constructive criticism offers positive feedback. Both analyze and evaluate, but constructive criticism gives solutions and seeks to improve. The world of critique has opened up in a huge way in the last twenty years. People's ever-growing platforms have deputized critics whose qualifications have not been proven. Everyone has a right to their opinion, but some people make it their duty to be negative and fundamentally disagreeable. So, recognize when and how comparison can help in a positive way. That's why honest constructive criticism is so important.

It takes wisdom to navigate through comparison. You have to be honest with yourself first and choose the right people to compare yourself to. The beginning hobby level artist should not compare themself to an expert level artist. Don't get me wrong—that is certainly a level you can aspire to attain. But you will need to choose contemporaries who are closer to your level of skill and achievement to compare yourself to in a healthy way. Use comparison to gauge what you are doing right and what you are doing wrong.

RESPONSE

Today, go to someone you trust and ask for feedback on a creative project. Don't take it personally when others see something in your work that can improve. Take what you can use and disregard what you know is not valuable.

takeA step back

18
Resetting

When I was growing up, video games were how my siblings and I got along. Don't get me wrong, they also started many arguments among my older brothers. But video games and attending church ultimately managed to keep us out of trouble. Back then we had a Super Nintendo and later a Nintendo 64. My brothers were intense gamers. My brother Nehemiah told me they would go to the grocery store and write down cheat codes from *Tips & Tricks* magazine. Cheat codes predated the widespread use of the internet and were usually shared in gaming magazines or comic books.

When something went wrong and the game glitched, my brothers would reset the console. If that didn't work, they would hit it on their knee and blow into the cartridge like they were playing the harmonica. Their breath removed dust from the cartridges to enable smoother function.

How much more powerful is God's breath? God's breath is not just hot air, and it truly enables us to reset. It is his *pneuma*, a Greek word that refers to his breath, his Spirit, the force that is unseen but ever present and ever active. This pneuma flows in and through us. (My artistic moniker is Numa Nate.)

If we look at God's creation as pieces of art, his creation on earth alone would be the largest and most robust creative series of all time. If we consider humanity alone, there are currently over eight billion people and counting. Out of these eight billion people, not one fingerprint is the same, even among identical twins. God's creativity and diversity extend even further if we look at plants and wildlife.

In a sense, God's breath reset the shape he made out of clay. His breath brought Adam to life, kind of like how my brothers' game cartridges came back to life after they blew on them. In other words, the creative power of God's breath repurposed a lump of dirt into a living soul.

Since the day God breathed the breath of life into Adam and he became a living soul, that same breath has been passed down from generation to generation. It's estimated that 117 billion people have been on earth since that day up to today. That first dust model of Adam has reproduced after its kind since the beginning of time. What an awe-inspiring Creator!

If we revisit biblical creation, Scripture says that there was darkness on the face of the deep. The waters were already there and then were divided. So God not only created, but he also revitalized. Even in telling Adam and Eve to be fruitful and multiply, he encouraged them to replenish the earth, to participate in the work of rejuvenating creation.

IMPROVE YOUR ENVIRONMENT WITH ART

Art can reset a space. It can repurpose disparate materials and transform them into a coherent, appealing whole, and that new work of art can revitalize an environment.

I have a love for composite art, which involves layering different elements together to make a new work. I use a combination of photos, some mine and some not: ink, charcoal sketches, animal prints, rugged textures like those of buildings, and weathered concrete. Part of my method is double exposure and heavy use of vibrant colors to make things pop. These are all elements that never would have crossed paths unless repurposed in a composite piece.

Have you ever seen a home makeover show? I don't mean the ones that totally change the structure but the ones that reorganize and revitalize the same space to create something new. Fresh color and finding balance in a space can turn basic into beautiful. Artforms such as composite art, collage, and many forms of sculpting also take existing materials (sometimes shabby ones) and make something fresh out of them. They take a space and beautify it with creativity.

You have the ability to make your space better. Decorate it and make it something new. Reset your focus. How do you do this? By placing God in charge of your work: "Commit your works to the Lord [submit and trust them to Him], and your plans will succeed [if you respond to His will and guidance]" (Proverbs 16:3 AMP).

RESPONSE

Find some materials in your immediate environment and transform them into a work of art.

MAKE IT HAPPEN

19

Inspiration and Imagination

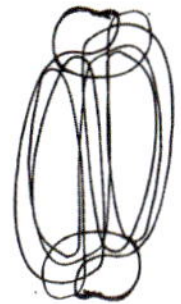

Creatively, it's important to possess imagination—the ability to see what things *can* become. Children naturally have that ability. As we grow, it's our job to make sure we don't lose it. I was ironing one day, and my four-year-old daughter said, "Hey, Dad, that ironing board kind of looks like a surfboard." Imagination connects things to each other. Imagination takes the raw and refines it. Imagination is being mentally stimulated to do or feel something, especially to do something creative. And if imagination is our *capacity* to envision new possibilities, then inspiration is the *force* that turns that vision into reality. Treat your imagination as more than a distracting daydream. Don't leave that idea in orbit. Fuel it and send it back to earth. Dr. Maya Angelou said, "A solitary fantasy can totally transform one million realities."[17]

The word *inspiration* has to do with the idea of drawing in breath. We only live because of inspiration: "And the Lord God formed man of the dust of the ground, and breathed into his nostrils the breath of life; and man became a living soul" (Genesis 2:7 KJV). It is through inspiration that we come alive.

Divine inspiration is inspiration that comes from God. The Word of God as a collection of books that we know as the Holy Bible is God-breathed. Though God didn't literally write the Holy Scriptures himself, he used holy and devout men and women to write what we consider to be the infallible written Word of God. So, the Word of God stems from God-given inspiration that moved the hearts of men and women. God partnered with these writers to get the job done by using their life experience, ethnicity, socioeconomic status, education, geographical locations, gender, and culture.

The Bible also shows God divinely inspiring people to create works of art, such as the artistic elements of the tabernacle. Divinely commissioned by God, the tabernacle was shown to Moses on the mount and was to be made from the recorded instructions in Exodus 25–31. The task was handed off to Bezaleel, the first man in Scripture who was referred to as being full of the Holy Ghost.

> And the Lord spake unto Moses, saying, "See, I have called by name Bezaleel the son of Uri, the son of Hur, of the tribe of Judah: And I have filled him with the Spirit of God, in wisdom, and in understanding, and in knowledge, and in all manner of workmanship, to devise cunning works, to work in gold, and in silver, and in brass, and in cutting of stones, to set them, and in carving of timber, to work in all manner of workmanship." (Exodus 31:1-5 KJV)

God gave Bezaleel everything he needed for the task at hand, including incredibly detailed instructions and raw materials. Bezaleel took the exhaustive list of materials like gold, silver, fine linen, and goat hair to make something intricate and spectacular. God had also equipped him with knowledge and understanding. Bezaleel was a cunning man filled with creativity from on high.[18] His work ethic, insight, and ingenuity glorified God.

Bezaleel proved to operate in excellence when it came to the artistry of the tabernacle and its construction. He was empowered by the Holy Spirit to do this task. Though he had no experience making a tabernacle, he was inspired to get it done and was ready to respond to the call.

The tabernacle, constructed with the work of Bezaleel's hands, was designated as the temporary dwelling place for God. In the same way, if you make a space for God in your work, he will come in and dwell there. He will shine through, and people will see the difference.

CREATIVE CONTROL

God inspires believers, those who follow Christ, to carry out his will on earth. The Holy Spirit empowers men, women, boys, and girls to do great things. Just as God partnered with people to write his Word, he also grants us certain liberties in creative expression—because a partnership is a mutually active endeavor. Just as the apostle Paul said, he spoke some things "by permission" (1 Corinthians 7:6 KJV). Paul is qualifying what he is about to say. He mentions this as a concession and not as an absolute command. He felt as though he had been granted the liberty to mention his own personal preference. Perhaps God did not put the writer's pen to paper, but there was an orchestration of divine destiny.

In his work of inspiration, God has given us a great deal of creative control. He has entrusted us to finish what he's inspired us to do. Our job now is to carry it out to the best of our ability. The most important thing to discover is that the ideas don't start with us, but we have the opportunity to do with them as we will. We could bury them, but what good would that do? We could postpone them, but that would be forfeiting obedience to the one who inspires us. Instead, it's best to yield to the creative impulse that God insists on. We don't control what comes to us and when, but we can control what we do with it.

Do you know the difference between a translator and an interpreter? A translator transfers written communication from one language to another, while an interpreter translates between languages in real time. We are to take the inspiration given to us by God in the way of our thoughts and interpret it into art and creative works.

God doesn't need to look around to inspire his imagination—he is the very source of imagination. And he gave an imagination to us. If he has placed something in your mind and it won't leave, that's your cue to work on making it happen. Push past the point of impossibility. Your imagination should cause you to dream big, to look beyond what you see to what *can* be. Home in on what's in front of you and think about what it can become. Take the limits of possibility off. Imagine yourself breaking the glass ceiling of what has already been established. You'll know when you find it. It may start as a thought. It may be an encounter or something you take in that creates a subtle curiosity. At other times it'll hit you like a ton of bricks. Inspiration and the way we find it all come from God.

Imagination is necessary for creativity. Creative people don't just see with their eyes. They see with their imagination. It is your mind's tendency to follow the curiosity of what-ifs. Curiosity may have killed the cat, but it cures the creative. Investigate new concepts and new ideas. Get a fresh perspective on something conventional—it is all within your reach. This gift to form new things is powerful when combined with wisdom and skill and a perception of what works well. You are not just tinkering around in the dark. You are bringing a needed light to situations and settings that need your input. When God inspires you to do something, you should act on it. He could have given it to eight billion other people, but he gave it to you. He spoke to your heart. It is our responsibility to turn inspiration into art.

RESPONSE

Take an existing concept and reimagine it.

Yes Lord

20

Divine Instruction

The crafting of the ark was a display of mastery and human translation of divine instructions. The ark did not suddenly materialize; its construction was facilitated by Noah based on God's instructions. Noah was a steward of what God inspired him to do. Though the blueprint came from God, who sits in eternity, it was Noah's responsibility to get it done in time. He had to manage the workload and the workforce—in this case, his sons. He was told which raw materials to use and how to use them. God gave him the details down to the exact dimensions. Some might say the detailed instructions made it easy, but I say they only added more pressure.

Being creative is not just about having talent or natural ability. Being skilled is one thing, but you have to put those skills into practice. God has given you a unique gift to make new things appear and to make existing things new. Being a creative person means you've been entrusted with ideas. Wherever I am and whatever I lend myself to, I'm giving ideas, whether it's through church administration, the student government association, or the PTA. Organizations value good ideas. Your creative impulse means that you are a thinker. Your value is not just in what you have done but also in your tendency to offer great ideas. Your mind is a safe place for ideas to develop into more. You can allow your ideas to become plans and your plans to become implementation.

MIDCENTURY MODERN GEO SHAPES

In these pieces I use clean lines and geometric shapes. This wall art provides a design style that offers a minimalist aesthetic.

God speaks through visions, dreams, people, his work, prayer and meditation, and your thoughts. What a privilege to erect what God directly instructed. What a joy to follow the blueprint given directly to you. When instruction hits us in such a direct way, we have to respond to it.

Inspiration is more abstract in nature. It prompts us to act, but the how and the what are less concrete. The result is left up to us to execute with a level of creative control. But when we receive God's instruction, it is concrete. The what and the how are all rolled out. If we skip a step, the structure may not work as intended. God's instruction expresses his will and something specific that he wants to do on earth.

OBEDIENCE

Our obedience should be our first response to divine instruction. Our posture before God should be yes, because the best response to divine instruction is holy compliance. When God gives a clear set of directives, it cuts out the guesswork. We can find out what we need and start. Even before we have what we need, we can begin by documenting what we heard or saw so no aspect of it is lost. I don't want any idea to slip through my fingers because I failed to jot it down. If I don't have access to one of my idea books I make a note in my phone, or if I'm driving I have Siri make a note.

Even if you don't know how to get it done, start. Build this ark to preserve what God made known to you in the moment of instruction. When God divinely instructs, nothing can afford to be lost in translation. Don't let hesitation be the factor that blocks the clarity of the instructions.

RESPONSE

How does God speak to you? Spend some time in prayer and reflection asking for divine instruction.

21

RESPONSIBILITY

CREATIVITY OFTEN SERVES as a great response to current events, whether for good or ill. The 1915 film *Birth of a Nation* by D. W. Griffith was a powerful tool of propaganda. Griffith brought his friend Thomas Dixon Jr.'s novel *The Clansman: A Historical Romance of the Ku Klux Klan* to the screen. This evil fantasy was translated to a film that created a destructive and deceiving narrative. Propagandistic devices like this film caused racial massacres like the Red Summer of 1919.[19] The call to action was clear: hate. This art was damaging. The divisive result was the resurgence of the Ku Klux Klan and the murder of innocent African Americans.[20] Although it was only misleading propaganda, it provoked adverse reactions and ushered in an era of unjustified murder and lynching in America. Recruiting for the Klan also skyrocketed after its release.[21]

Creations with destructive intentions leave space for righteous responses that can be equally powerful. Oscar Micheaux responded in kind with his 1920 film *Within Our Gates*, which rivaled the stereotypes of *Birth of a Nation*. He took upon himself the responsibility to combat this popular film that received so much notoriety and fueled the forces of racism. *Within Our Gates* provided a responsive narrative to the damaging stereotypes and gross misinformation of *Birth of a Nation*, showing the humanity of Black people in a realistic landscape of character, wit, and diversity.

Creativity can be a defender. It can be a force to spark cultural change or at least start the conversation. In this case, creativity aided hate in a smear campaign against a race of people by spreading damaging ideas and propaganda. But creativity can and should be a force for good. Micheaux highlighted the humanity of the people in his film through non-stereotypical representation and their individual personalities. Black people were not depicted as the scum of the earth but as protagonists and antagonists who owned the story.

Like Micheaux, we have a responsibility to make a meaningful impact with our art. Our art affects those who experience it. Subject matter has the power to persuade for good or bad, inform, and inspire ideals.

Satire can inform in a way that is artistic and clever, conveying serious ideas that otherwise wouldn't be heard. Art gives us the freedom to discuss controversial ideas.

CATALYZING CHANGE

In the 1960s, America was coming of age and dealing with catastrophic things like assassinations and war. The social landscape was changing, and the revolution was literally being televised. Artists decided not to keep quiet and instead took up arms to say with their art what Muhammad Ali and others said: Empty and unfounded hate is wrong.

Artistic works provide social commentary. Creativity can help you escape a contrasting existence, but there comes a time when you must choose not to escape and address what you see around you. The more tumultuous the times, the more opportunities present themselves to address what's going on. I agree with American singer, musician, and civil rights activist Nina Simone, who stated her views on the obligation of an artist. Simone lent her voice in an uncompromising way to the causes of her day. Her music was just as much a part of her activism as any of her other efforts. She used it to celebrate, she used it to mourn, and she used it to protest. In her words, "An artist's duty as far as I'm concerned is to reflect the times. I think that is true of painters, sculptors, poets, musicians. As far as I'm concerned, it's their choice. But I choose to reflect the times and situations in which I find myself." Simone goes on to say, "How can you be an artist and not reflect the times? That to me is a definition of an artist."[22] Your superpower is to convey feeling into art. Use your superpower to send a message that will spark ideas, which will then spark change in society. Let your work be the catalyst for change.

My art seeks to lift the misunderstood and underrepresented. I choose to empower the next generation. I also use my art to celebrate and protest. I release my art into the world so more joy can be here. I protest visually so it cannot be unseen. I celebrate those who often go overlooked or underappreciated. In choosing to express myself this way, I seek to tear down walls that divide people. I confront negative ideas because it is within my power to do so, not only in my celebration of Black people and Black culture but also in my efforts to allow us all to understand each other better. All that experience my art, though with varying degrees of perception and perspective, have the opportunity to hold a shared experience.

PAPER PORTRAITS

Paper Portraits are a nod to the everyday people with extraordinary drive who inspire me daily. The poet, the musical therapist, the bivocational pastor all have left indelible marks on me as we have crossed paths. How does one measure success? Is it passion, notoriety, or authenticity? These are all African American people who are either emerging leaders or unsung heroes, people who have defied the odds or are currently navigating through the obstacles of life with hope, passion, perseverance, character, and divine inspiration. This series aims to celebrate those people.

Art can enable you to become a prophetic voice, much like a preacher. But your pulpit is bigger. You can preach in art galleries, in museums, on the big screen, and in the homes of hundreds of millions of people. Documenting the times. Creating social commentary. Capturing the essence of culture and being a mirror to an otherwise blinded society.

The response to my creative impulse is part of my worship to God. I dedicate and give back to him what he has given to me. What I create are gifts to the world that bear his mark of what he has given me to share.

CREATIVE BOUNDARIES

Art is an expression of the human spirit—and that spirit is all over the place at times. This is due to varying opinions, views, and standards of morality. That's why we need to have parameters around our creative behavior and know what to subscribe to or not. Just as there is godly creation, there is ungodly creation. If we want God to breathe on what we create, it should be pleasing to him. Remember, God breathes into things that look like him.

If the work that you do does not line up with your belief system, you will never be at peace. What use is making a lot of money but not being able to reconcile to your own conscience? Lucrative doesn't always mean logical. Christian artists have a responsibility to be light and salt in a dark world. Our work should stand out in subject matter, impact, and excellence.

We as Christians also must be careful about the artistic appropriation of the image of God. Christ's image has been hijacked. Idolatry and pride have made a Jesus who doesn't resemble the Jesus of Nazareth. We are made in the image of God, but we seem to have made a god in the image of us. Warner Sallman's painting *Head of Christ* has traveled the world over since 1940. This painting is considered a famous depiction of Jesus. But for many people of color, it is an infamous and damaging work of art. If you close your eyes to imagine Jesus and see a white man with a sandy brown beard, the effects of this work of art and many like it are to blame.

Can you understand the frustration of people of color who research a biblical figure online and are bombarded with images that are historically inaccurate? I don't think Sallman was doing something intentionally diabolical here. He perhaps thought he was expressing himself through creative worship. However, his artistic expression has likely been damaging to many people's self-esteem and God-consciousness. Works like these have marginalized the imagination of many who seek to envision God without societal bias.

Sallman would travel to churches and tell his wife and the congregants, "Sing to me about Jesus," before he painted one of his works of art.[23] In a contemporary context, this scene reminds me of worship services I've attended, where an artist would have an easel and a paintbrush and interpret the service through a work of art, most commonly a painting. They would start painting at the beginning of the service and depict the subject matter of the sermon topic at the end of the service, through an act of divine inspiration. Sallman's situation shows us that even art created in good conditions with good intentions can have a negative impact, so we have to be very careful about how our art influences the world around us.

Though Sallman's paintings are among the most well-known religious images, his art may have had an unintended negative impact on many people. Griffith's artistic expression in *Birth of a Nation* was harmful to our society as well. But artists like Micheaux brought about positive change through creativity. Every creative person is responsible not only to create authentically but also to create art that makes the world a better place.

RESPONSE

Identify a cause that matters to you. Then jot down a few ideas on how to contribute to that cause with your art.

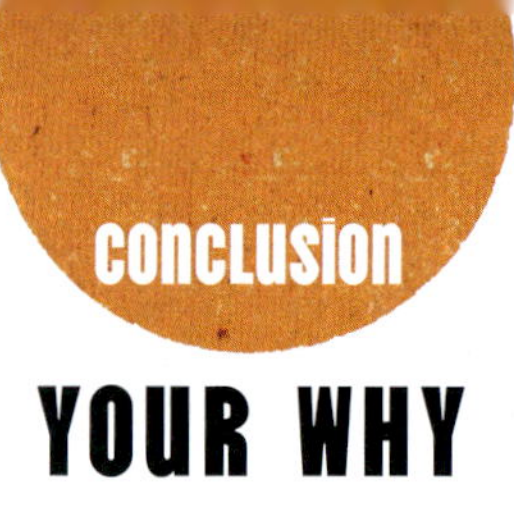

YOUR WHY

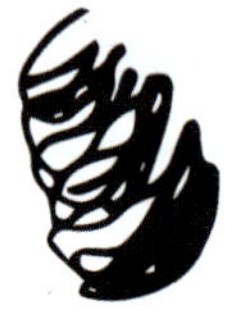

Your art is an extension of your voice. As the youngest of three boys with a stutter at times, I know the value of having a clear voice, particularly a distinct creative voice. It's important to convey ideas with clarity. As your ideas go out into the world, it is up to the audience to decide how to perceive your message.

Prayerfully, this book has helped you amplify your artistic voice. I pray that the biblical insights on collaboration, creation, and rest have equipped you to speak through your creations, and I pray my artwork has inspired you to speak even louder. After all, the One we're praying to spoke the artwork of creation into existence.

God's voice brought forth the light and our existence. The Word of God is personified as Jesus: "He is the image of the invisible God, the firstborn over all creation" (Colossians 1:15 NKJV). Christ was active in the creation process, which was a springing forth out of nothing. That's why finding *our* creative voice is so important. Doing so allows us to create work that forms a whole new world of possibilities. It is only by our voice that the world of our thoughts can become a reality. Even when we collaborate, we must actively participate to bring our ideas into being. God spoke and things started happening.

If we are to impact this world for good, we have to learn how to make our creative voices heard. Our art can go places that we might never visit and spark conversations that we might never hear.

Can we say for certain *why* God spoke the universe into existence? Theologians have been debating this question for millennia, and I don't pretend to have a definitive answer. But I agree with the many theologians who say God created because it pleased him. Scripture says we were made for God's pleasure. Everything was created because he wanted it: "You are worthy, our Lord and God, to receive glory and honor and power, because you created all things. It is by your will that they existed and were created" (Revelation 4:11 CEB).

Why are you creating? Is it for your pleasure? Is it your calling? Are you helping others? Whatever your "why" is, it should bring a level of fulfillment to you and your creative impulse.

The purpose of my art is to bring people together—that's the part about creativity that brings me the most joy. I'm collaborating with my audience to create a transformative experience. One of my creative mottos is, "Make your mark." But for me, this is more than a motto; it is a call to action.

I have a dream of creating an engaging art exhibit. It would have different pieces of paper and other materials available, along with markers, pens, charcoal sticks, and Conté crayons. Participants would be encouraged to make an abstract mark with their materials of choice and even initial their mark if they desired. The resulting marks would be rearranged to make another composition for every instance and installation of the exposition. The fun part would be for participants to revisit the exhibit and see if they could identify their mark. As the exhibit travels and circulates, it would get bigger. All those marks would create something ever growing and ever changing. The abstract strokes of many would become something beautiful. The big picture of my work is to encourage people to make their mark with their God-given individuality in whatever arena they occupy—celebrating their divine inspiration, their sacred purpose, and the freedom to be themselves. My work seeks to provide inspiration for life.

Do you have a big creative dream like this? Who's in your corner who can collaborate with you? What rhythms of rest do you need to implement to help make your dream a reality? How can you make your mark? The world is waiting to hear your voice.

MAKE
YOUR
MARK

ACKNOWLEDGMENTS

PRANIECE. YOU INSPIRE ME with your courage and excellence every day. Thank you for loving me. You make my heart smile. I still haven't seen anything as beautiful as you. Keep blazing your own trail. You are truly remarkable.

To my beautiful daughter, Zuri. You keep me laughing and amaze me with your strength and resilience. You will forever be my miracle and proof that God loves me. You bring Daddy joy.

Ezra. Daddy's helper. I love you, son. Not only did you steal my face, but you've stolen my heart from day one. Your kindness and thoughtfulness inspire me every day. I'm excited about both of your futures.

Mom. My creative brain was passed down from you. I hope this book reignites your flame of creativity most of all. Your creative voice is needed. Thank you for your love and always being there for me. Thank you for how you have modeled a Christlike life for so many.

Atlas Jr. You started the trend of designers in our family, and I'm forever grateful for your courageous step to the Career Center. Your creativity and passion are unmatched. Never stop dreaming. Never stop creating. Never stop believing.

Nehemiah, thanks for always leading me in the right direction. You gave me the tools to do well in ministry and design. I followed your model for so much in life.

My nieces and nephews, whom I love so dearly. Let this book inspire you to dream unimaginable possibilities. You have the opportunity to do amazing things in life. Seize it and let nothing turn you around.

Creations

DIGITAL ABSTRACT

- Soul Maze
- Purple Play
- Spot 1
- Ink Paint
- I Shall
- Blue Ink
- Pink Orbs
- Golden Crayon

LIFTED SCRIBBLE

- Golden Flower
- If My People
- Blue Light
- Black Rose Gold
- Black & Bloom 2
- BlackGirlJoy
- St. Louis
- 207, New York
- Dreamer
- Petty-n-Pink
- 206, Close up Square
- Open Heaven
- 52.7
- Black & Bloom
- Hezekiah
- Winter Flower
- Untitled, 10.28.24
- Black & Bloom 3

ABSTRACT INK STROKES

- Noir Abstract 1
- Noir Abstract 2
- Vector Island
- Bash 1
- BluBlack

MIDCENTURY MODERN GEO SHAPES

- Midcentury Spheres 2.1
- Midcentury Spheres 2.2
- Midcentury Spheres 4
- Curo 1
- Curo 2

PAPER PORTRAITS

- PaperPreacher
- PaperSpeach
- Paper Portrait#012
- Paper Pastor
- Paper Bean
- PaperWarrior
- Increase

Paint Flower

NOTES

[1] "Bob Ross on the Phil Donahue Show," interview by Phil Donahue, *The Phil Donahue Show*, aired April 1994, YouTube, www.youtube.com/shorts/z9_CfZZtINo.

[2] "Form Follows Function: Principles and Impact on Architecture," *DesignHorizons*, July 2, 2024, www.designhorizons.org.

[3] *Rose Book of Bible Charts, Maps, and Time Lines*, 10th anniv. ed. (Rose Publishing LLC, Hendrickson Publishers, 2015).

[4] "Numbers of Insects (Species and Individuals)," Information Sheet Number 18, 1996, *Smithsonian*, www.si.edu/spotlight/buginfo/bugnos.

[5] "List of Beetles," Britannica, last updated April 14, 2025, www.britannica.com/animal/list-of-beetles-2072991.

[6] *Hollywood Shuffle* is an American satirical comedy film about African Americans being depicted with racial stereotypes in film and televisions. Directed by Robert Townsend and written by Keenen Ivory Wayans and Robert Townsend (The Samuel Goldwyn Company, MGM, 1987).

[7] Keenen Ivory Wayans from *The Black List: Volume 1*, directed by Timothy Greenfield-Sanders, aired 2008, HBO, YouTube, www.youtube.com/watch?v=rsZYZMEdLOo.

[8] Myles Munroe, *The Spirit of Leadership: Cultivating the Attributes That Influence Human Action* (Whitaker House, 2005). Kindle.

[9] "How Ice Cream Is Made," Modern Marvels, season 14, episode 18, created by Bruce Nash, aired on June 3, 2008, History Channel, www.history.com/shows/modern-marvels/season-14/episode-18.

[10] Starr Anderson, "EnChroma-Adapted Viewfinders have Been Installed at All Virginia State Parks," Virginia Department of Conservation and Recreation, August 7, 2024, www.dcr.virginia.gov/state-parks/blog/enchroma-adapted-viewfinders-have-been-installed-at-all-virginia-state-parks.

[11] *Conversations with Maya Angelou*, ed. Jeffrey M. Elliot (University Press of Mississippi, 1989).

[12] *Do the Right Thing*, A 1989 comedy-drama film directed by Spike Lee about the escalating racial tensions in a Brooklyn neighborhood on a hot summer day (Universal Pictures).

[13] Thomas A. Dorsey, "Precious Lord, Take My Hand," 1932.

[14] Natasha Smith, *Can You Just Sit with Me? Healthy Grieving for the Losses of Life* (InterVarsity Press, 2023).

[15] Jonathan Dean, "Denzel Washington: 'I Made Some Real Clunkers after Malcolm X,'" *The Sunday Times*, Times Media Limited, November 15, 2024, www.thetimes.com/culture/film/article/denzel-washington-gladiator-ii-interview-ls9dv88qw.

[16] Martin Luther King Jr., quoted in *The Words of Martin Luther King, Jr.*, ed. Coretta Scott King (Newmarket Press, 1983).

[17] Maya Angelou, *The Heart of a Woman* (Random House, 1981), 189.

[18] Herbert Lockyer, *All the Men of the Bible* (Zondervan, 1988), 76.

[19] The summer after World War I ended, white mobs across the Midwest and South terrorized Black communities, destroying property and killing or injuring hundreds of Black people. This period in history is known as the Red Summer.

[20] "Red Summer of 1919," Equal Justice Initiative, October 28, 2019, https://eji.org/news/history-racial-injustice-red-summer-of-1919/.

[21] Alexis Clark, "How 'The Birth of a Nation' Revived the Ku Klux Klan," History, A+E Global Media, May 28, 2025, www.history.com/articles/kkk-birth-of-a-nation-film.

[22] Lou House, "Nina Simone Interview," *Black Journal*, season 1, episode 38, National Educational Television, October 27, 1969, YouTube, www.youtube.com/watch?v=JcVrbRaNLxY.

[23] Cathy Norman Peterson, "Grappling with the Image of Jesus," The Evangelical Covenant Church, January 16, 2024, https://covchurch.org/2024/01/16/grappling-with-the-image-of-jesus/.